What Is Society?

THE PINE FORGE PRESS SOCIAL SCIENCE LIBRARY

The McDonaldization of Society: An Investigation Into the Changing Character of Contemporary Social Life *by George Ritzer*

Sociological Snapshots: Seeing Social Structure and Change in Everyday Life *by Jack Levin*

What Is Society? Reflections on Freedom, Order, and Change *by Earl Babbie*

The Production of Reality: Essays and Readings in Social Psychology *by Peter Kollock and Jodi O'Brien*

Adventures in Social Research: Data Analysis Using SPSS$^{®}$ *by Earl Babbie and Fred Halley*

Crime and Everyday Life: Insights and Implications for Society *by Marcus Felson*

Sociology of Work: Perspectives, Analyses, Issues *by Richard H. Hall*

Aging: Concepts and Controversies *by Harry R. Moody, Jr.*

Worlds of Difference: Structured Inequality and the Aging Experience *by Eleanor Palo Stoller and Rose Campbell Gibson*

Forthcoming

Sociology for a New Century *A Pine Forge Press Series edited by Charles Ragin, Wendy Griswold, and Larry Griffin*

- **Social Psychology and Social Institutions** *by Denise D. and William T. Bielby*
- **The Social Ecology of Natural Resources and Development** *by Stephen G. Bunker*
- **How Societies Change** *by Daniel Chirot*
- **Ethnic Dynamics in the Modern World: Continuity and Transformation** *by Stephen Cornell*
- **Sociology of Childhood** *by William A. Corsaro*
- **Cultures and Societies in a Changing World** *by Wendy Griswold*
- **Crime and Disrepute: Comparative Perspectives** *by John Hagan*
- **Racism and the Modern World: Sociological Perspectives** *by Wilmot James*
- **Waves of Democracy** *by John Markoff*
- **Organizations in a World Economy** *by Walter W. Powell*
- **Constructing Social Research** *by Charles C. Ragin*
- **Women, Men, and Work** *by Barbara Reskin and Irene Padavic*
- **Cities in a World Economy** *by Saskia Sassen*

What Is Society?

*Reflections on
Freedom, Order, and Change*

Earl R. Babbie

PINE FORGE PRESS

Thousand Oaks ▪ London ▪ New Delhi

Dedicated to Laurence J. Peter,
who saw the cosmic joke embedded in so much
of our social structure and couldn't resist telling his friends.

Copyright © 1994 by Pine Forge Press

For information, address:

Pine Forge Press
A Sage Publications Company
2455 Teller Road
Thousand Oaks, California 91320

Copy Editor: Linda Poderski
Text Design: Lisa Mirski
Cover Design: Paula Shuhert
Proofreader: Karen Axelton
Typesetter: Christina Hill
Printer: Publishers Press
Sage Production Editor: Judith L. Hunter

Printed in the United States of America

1 2 3 4 5 6 7 8 9 10—98 97 96 95 94

Library of Congress Cataloging-in-Publication Data

Babbie, Earl R.
    What is society? : reflections on freedom, order, and
change /
    Earl R. Babbie.
        p. cm.
    Includes bibliographical references and index.
    ISBN 0-8039-9015-4 (pbk.)
    1. Social structure. 2. Sociology.   I. Title
HM131.B133 1994
301—dc20   93-15178
                                                        CIP

CONTENTS

About the Author

Earl Babbie was born in Detroit, Michigan, in 1938, though he grew up in Vermont and New Hampshire. In 1956, he set off for Harvard Yard, where he spent the next 4 years learning more than he initially had planned. After 3 years with the United States Marine Corps, mostly in Asia, Babbie began graduate studies at the University of California, Berkeley. He received his Ph.D. from Berkeley in 1969. Babbie taught sociology at the University of Hawaii from 1968 through 1979, took time off from teaching and research to write full-time for 8 years, and then joined the faculty at Chapman University in Southern California in 1987. Although an author of numerous research articles and monographs, Babbie is best known for the many texts he has written that have been widely adopted in colleges throughout the United States and the world. Babbie also has been active in the American Sociological Association for 25 years and currently serves on the ASA's governing council. He has been married to his wife, Sheila, for 27 years, and they have a son, Aaron, who aspires to a career in writing.

About the Publisher

Pine Forge Press is a new educational publisher, dedicated to publishing innovative books and software throughout the social sciences. On this and any other of our publications, we welcome your comments, ideas, and suggestions. Please call or write to

Pine Forge Press
A Sage Publications Company
2455 Teller Road
Thousand Oaks, CA 91320
805-499-4224
Internet: sdr@pfp.sagepub.com

Despite the fact that you may have been assigned this book in a college course, I would very much like you to enjoy it. I had that in mind when I wrote it.

The topic of this book is something quite unusual, actually. You can't see it, hear it, touch it, taste it, or feel it, and yet it controls much of your life. It would be useful for you to understand something like that, but it obviously will take a special way of looking and listening.

The strange phenomenon I am talking about is called *social structure* (otherwise termed *society*), and the special way of looking and listening is called *sociology*. In this book, you will take a peek inside the invisible world of norms, sanctions, values, and beliefs that shape what we think and feel, as well as how we behave. I hope the book will shed some light into corners of life that may have puzzled you from time to time. It should draw your attention to aspects of society that you have never really thought about. Maybe you will find them as fascinating as we sociologists do. Although much of this book points to problems in the functioning of society, that is only part of the picture. I also want you to see how the structure of society makes our lives together possible. And, most important, I would like you to see that it is possible to *change* those aspects of society that are not working the way they should. The toolbox for that latter job is called *sociology*.

This book has another special meaning for me. It was the first book signed for publication with a new publishing company: Pine Forge Press. Twenty years ago, Steve Rutter was the new sociology editor at Wadsworth Publishing Company. That same year, I signed a contract to write my first textbook, *Survey Research Methods*, with Wadsworth. Because we were both new to the job, Steve and I had to make up the craft of building books together. It was the kind of partnership I suspect authors and editors seldom have the privilege to experience. Steve began as my editor and ended as my brother. As Steve's career in publishing changed, a side effect was that we ceased working side by side. As blessed as I have been with the editors who have succeeded him, I have missed Steve telling me what he thought was wrong with what I had written, my grumbling about this criticism, and then rewriting along the lines he suggested, finally discovering what it was I had tried to say in the first place. This book has meant an opportunity to work one-on-one together, and I have loved it (even if he still does demand too much). Steve has been ably assisted in this venture by Chiara Huddleston. Chiara, in turn, has been assisted by an excellent production team: Linda Poderski, copy editor; Judith Hunter, production editor; Karen Axelton, proofreader; and Christina Hill, typesetter.

Although I take personal responsibility for everything you will find in the pages to follow, I do want to acknowledge the powerful guidance and suggestions I have received from the following colleagues, who have commented on various drafts of the book: Paul J. Baker, Illinois State University; Dan Chambliss, Hamilton College; Paula J. Dubeck, University of Cincinnati; Melvyn Fein, Kennesaw State College; Barry Goetz, University of California at Los Angeles; Anne Hastings, University of North Carolina at Chapel Hill; Kichiro Iwamoto, Santa Clara University; Mary Ann Maguire, Tulane University; Charles O'Connor, Bemidji State University; Tim Schaefer, Central Michigan University; Richard L. Simpson, University of North Carolina at Chapel Hill; Marc Ventresca, University of Illinois; John Walsh, University of Illinois; and Idee Winfield, Louisiana State University.

I have dedicated this book to my friend Laurence J. Peter, whose death in January 1989 kept me from sharing the finished product with him. Laurence devoted much of his career to drawing our attention to the foibles of organized social life. Many of his insights are preserved in his 1969 best-seller *The Peter Principle*, which immortalized his observation that in any hierarchy, individuals rise to their levels of incompetence. Laurence thought that was pretty funny, and he also thought poking fun at such dysfunctions was a good step toward changing them. One of his friends, Matt Wueker, once drew a cartoon of a hapless Laurence being confronted at the Pearly Gates by Saint Peter, who apologized, "Sorry, Dr. Peter. We seem to have lost your paperwork." As things turned out, his official death certificate had five errors in it. I think Laurence would have thought that was pretty funny too.

CHAPTER ONE

Introducing an Unusual Entity

There is a dimension of reality that is invisible and unrecognized by most people, and yet it controls our lives in many ways. In this introduction, we first confront the entity to which some say we owe our souls.

For many years, I have participated in The Holiday Project, an organization formed in 1973 around the idea of visiting institutionalized people—in hospitals, mental wards, convalescent homes, prisons, and so on—during the Christmas and Hanukkah holidays. It began with a handful of people in San Francisco, and it expanded over time. In recent years, some 20,000 people in dozens of cities across the country have visited about 200,000 shut-ins annually.

The Holiday Project was founded on a principle or purpose that was and is, I think, intrinsically good. Who but the most mean-spirited grinch could object to visiting shut-ins during the holidays? Not surprisingly, both the visitors and the visitees (sociologists talk that way, sometimes) have had warm, satisfying, even magical experiences through The Holiday Project.

In the early years, a group of 10 to 20 of us would decide to visit a particular institution. We'd each chip in a few dollars for some presents. Initially we had a limit of $3 apiece because the project wasn't about how much money you could give. We said it was about giving yourself. Some in the group would buy and wrap the presents—perfume, socks, things like that—and others would make arrangements with the institution. On the day of the visit, somebody would bring song sheets.

We'd usually meet in the parking lot half an hour or so in advance of the visit, practice our singing—which probably could have profited from more practice—and then we'd invade the institution, singing songs with the shut-ins, giving them presents, talking with them, listening to them, and, most important, simply being with them during a time when being together was in the air and many of them were feeling alone.

The Holiday Project is a great embodiment of what we sometimes speak of as "the human spirit." It's an idea that deserved to succeed, and it has. At the same time, I've been in a position to see something else develop, also called The Holiday Project, which is quite different from what I've been describing in such glowing terms. This other Holiday Project, though not evil or malicious (this is not an exposé), reflects on the subject of this book.

Although my experience of The Holiday Project visits over the years has been uniformly rewarding and joyous, I've also found myself frustrated from time to time. As the good idea became formally organized, incorporated, and regulated as a charitable organization under the laws of California, minor annoyances cropped up from time to time. Whereas we initially chipped in a few bucks, we began to receive requests from headquarters (there was now a headquarters) for regular financial reporting. How much money had been raised? What was the value of anything contributed by merchants? How was the money spent? (Please include receipts.)

Soon somebody somewhere was assigning us to institutions and informing us of the time and place to assemble. Instead of being limited to contributions of $3, we soon were encouraged to give more generously—not just for presents, but for the costs of administering the organization. From time to time, we'd have a fund-raising idea that would be vetoed by headquarters, with an explanation that it might jeopardize our tax-exempt status, that it might expose the organization to a liability risk, or other similar reasons. Increasingly the participants in The Holiday Project would complain that much of our time and effort seemed devoted to things that had nothing to do with the intention and experience that brought us together in the first place.

So far, what I have said about the evolution of The Holiday Project might sound like the beginnings of a sensational exposé of individual wrongdoing and shame. None of that will follow. Not only was The Holiday Project founded on a pure and wonderful idea, but the people I met in it at all levels also are among the most dedicated I have ever known. The something amiss here is not a function of individual human beings.

After several years of participating in local visits, I was asked to serve on the national Board of Directors of The Holiday Project, and I did so for several years. It was one of the most satisfying experiences I have had. I had a chance to make a real contribution to the well-being and happiness of others and to work side by side with other people committed to making such a contribution.

The point of this story about The Holiday Project, however, is that as a member of the Board of Directors, I found myself doing all of those things that I'd been annoyed by as a local participant. We were constantly harassing local committees to submit their monthly financial reports so that we could provide the auditors with what they needed to support our continuation as a charity under the laws of California.

I found myself worrying about liability. Should we continue to let local committees visit prisons? What if they were taken hostage? Could The Holiday Project be sued? A committee in Oakland wanted to hold a rock concert to raise money for the organization; but what if it lost money? Who would have to pay?

As the project grew in size, we found that we could no longer remain a totally volunteer organization. We hired an executive director, with a contract, a modest salary, and a budget for phone calls, supplies, and so forth. Having made that commitment, however, it was all the more important to guarantee a flow of income for the organization. That became the first responsibility of the executive director.

On reflection, my experience on the Board of Directors of The Holiday Project showed me that I couldn't explain the foibles of organizations solely in terms of human failings. Something more was at work. The answer had to lie in what an organization was.

THE THRILL IS OFTEN GONE

The phenomenon I have been outlining, using the Holiday Project as an illustration, operates in virtually all aspects of our lives. You and I have a host of experiences that delight us greatly and that seem important to us. They are so important, in fact, that we take steps to ensure their persistence. And in the process of organizing those experiences so as to guard them, we often seem to protect them to death.

Consider the experience of teaching/learning. I know you've more than once had that exhilarating experience of learning something. It may have been something you were struggling with, some puzzle that just seemed to be eluding you. Then *you got it!* We often refer to such moments as an "Aha! experience." When you've had such an experience, you probably feel on top of the world for a while.

Teaching someone—or more properly, helping someone learn—can be equally satisfying. When you can thrill to someone else's Aha! experience and know that you had a hand in bringing it about, that's the kind of thing that leads people to seek careers as teachers. You've had experiences like that whether or not you ever wanted to become a teacher.

Given the thrill of such experiences, it's no wonder that we establish organizations devoted to keeping the thrill alive. We call them schools, colleges, and universities. The sad thing, however, is that although the excitement of teaching and learning occurs in such organizations, it is hardly typical.

Imagine what it would be like if students and teachers in our schools were having an unending series of experiences such as those I just described. We'd have to keep the doors open 24 hours a day; the students wouldn't want to go home. The teachers would neglect their families and forget to pick up their paychecks. These are not the problems people commonly speak of when they bemoan the "crisis in education."

We do the same with loving relationships. I hope you've had the experience of being deeply and truly in love. If so, you've probably gone through periods of time when you couldn't concentrate on anything other than your true love. You may have forgotten appointments, even forgotten to eat, or had trouble sleeping.

Every day, people find themselves so much in love that they decide to safeguard their love by getting married. Although many of them enjoy years of passion and love, it would be an overstatement to say that these things are assured. In recent years in the United States, we've had half as many divorces as marriages each year. And many of the marriages that last can hardly be described as continuous experiences of love and devotion.

There are countless other examples of this phenomenon that we might examine. You might contrast a deeply powerful religious experience with the routine experience of attending organized worship services. Contrast the pride of achievement sometimes experienced in a job well done with the drudgery that so often typifies modern work.

This is not to say that organizing or organizations are bad; sometimes they provide the site for such experiences. But very often the act of organizing seems to kill the experience that may have brought us together in the first place. That is the phenomenon I want to delve into in this book. To do so, I am going to ask some unusual questions and perhaps uncover some even more unusual answers.

A STRANGE HUMAN CREATION

What is an organization or a society made of? Perhaps the answer that comes most readily to mind is "people." An organization is some kind of collection of human beings, and so is a society. Although this answer is certainly correct in a way, it also misses something very important. The book you have just opened is dedicated to uncovering and revealing the something that the obvious answer misses.

A society or an organization is, I suggest, something more—I prefer to say something *other* than the individual human beings who comprise it at any given time. As partial evidence in support of this assertion, notice that societies typically outlast any of the individual women and men who create and pass through them, and many organizations achieve this endurance as well.

The Roman Catholic Church as an organized religion is arguably about 2,000 years old. The clan of the cave bear, never incorporated as far as I know, lasted for some 10,000 years. When Herman Hollerith founded the Tabulating Machine Company in 1896, he set something in motion that would be alive and well nearly 100 years later and would be known as International Business Machines: IBM.

The United States of America is more than 200 years old. Or consider this: Something we call the United States Senate has been in existence for more than 200 years. That something is easily older than any individual U.S. Senator. The question we will address is: What exactly is that something that outlasted Daniel Webster and Henry Clay and will outlast all of those women and men serving in the Senate today?

Actually I want to address several questions about the whatever-it-is that organizations and societies are:

- What's their purpose for being?
- What are they made of?
- How is what they're made of structured?
- Why do they often become our adversaries?
- How can we regain control over them?

As you can imagine, the last two of these questions most prompted this book. When I say that organizations or societies become our adversaries, I am referring to all the ways we find our lives as individual human beings constrained and diminished by the organizations and societies we participate in and deal with. My opening discussion of The Holiday Project illustrates some of what I am talking about here. But it can get much worse.

Consider those times you found yourself hemmed in by rules and regulations that may have made sense sometime and might even still make sense in some situations but are clearly idiotic in your particular situation. Take a moment to reflect on experiences you may have had with such organizations as a post office, an insurance company, a college or university administration, the department of motor vehicles, a large supermarket chain, a mail-order book club, the military, and your local planning commission. Recall the last time someone said, "I don't make the rules, I just enforce them." This book is about those rules and how they seem to have a life of their own.

Georg Simmel, an earlier sociologist, saw this phenomenon in almost mystical terms, as he described the formation and growing independence of our social creations:

> Whenever life progresses beyond the animal level to that of spirit, and spirit progresses to the level of culture, an internal contradiction appears. . . . although these forms arise out of the life process, because of their unique constellation they do not share the restless rhythm of life . . . They acquire fixed identities, a logic and lawfulness of their own; this new rigidity inevitably places them at a distance from the spiritual dynamic which created them and which makes them independent.
>
> Life, as we have said, can manifest itself only in particular forms; yet, owing to its essential restlessness, life constantly struggles against its own products, which have become fixed and do not move along with it. This process manifests itself as the displacement of an old form by a new one.
>
> Life as such is formless, yet incessantly generates forms for itself. As soon as each form appears, however, it demands a validity which transcends the moment and is emancipated from the pulse of life. For this reason, life is always in a latent opposition to the form. This tension soon expresses itself in this sphere and in that; eventually it develops into a comprehensive cultural necessity. (Simmel, 1921/1968, pp. 11-12)

Sociologists and psychologists often speak positively about people having a "sense of belonging," and we often study the cliques, organizations, and societies people belong to. This book focuses on the double meaning of the phrase *belong to*. There is a vast difference between a debutante belonging to a country club and a slave belonging to a master. It is the difference between membership and ownership.

Max Weber, one of the founders of modern sociology, is noted for his penetrating analysis of bureaucracy as a form of social organization. Although Weber was clear in describing the advantages of bureaucracy, he also warned that it could take on a life of its own, becoming an "iron cage" for those who serve in it.

After characterizing bureaucracy as being "among those social structures which are the hardest to destroy" and "practically unshatterable" as a power relationship, he continued:

The individual bureaucrat cannot squirm out of the apparatus in which he is harnessed. In contrast to the honorific or avocational "notable," the professional bureaucrat is chained to his activity by his entire material and ideal existence. In the great majority of cases, he is only a single cog in an ever-moving mechanism which prescribes to him an essentially fixed route of march. The official is entrusted with specialized tasks and normally the mechanism cannot be put into notion or arrested by him, but only from the very top. The individual bureaucrat is thus forged to the community of all the functionaries who are integrated into the mechanism. They have a common interest in seeing that the mechanism continues its functions and that the societally exercised authority carries on. (Weber, 1925/1946, pp. 228-229)

When I was young, country singer Tennessee Ernie Ford recorded a very popular song about the plight of coal miners forced to load a daily quota of "Sixteen Tons" of coal for meager pay. Moreover, each paycheck always went directly to the general store owned by the company, to pay for food and other necessities advanced on credit between paychecks. The song described a system in which miners could never get ahead of their debts to the store, and it kept ending on the refrain: "I owe my soul to the company store."

This is a book about "the company store." As we will see, our organizations and societies often operate like the company store in the song. Although they may provide us with much of what we need for survival, those benefits come at a cost.

To fully launch us into our inquiry, I propose a mental experiment that you may find useful. That experiment will reveal an overview of the investigation to follow throughout the remainder of the book.

THE FLOW OF HUMANITY

Imagine looking out a third- or fourth-story window in a large city, looking down on the flow of humanity below you. Although you can tell that you are looking at human beings walking along the sidewalks, crossing the street, and going in and out of buildings, it's easy to overlook the idiosyncratic qualities of each individual. Sometimes we joke about them looking like ants.

In your mind's eye, try to see the scurrying humans as a flow of material, something like those pictures you've seen of lava flowing down a hillside from an erupting volcano or water meandering across a vacant lot after a heavy rain. Notice that the movement is not random;

there are patterns to it, but the patterns are not altogether orderly and predictable.

Now imagine yourself as a participant in that flow of humanity—as you really are during much of your waking hours. If not on a city street, imagine yourself among the mass of students and faculty moving about a college campus. Most are walking along sidewalks and streets, though the occasional exceptions cut across lawns or even climb over low walls. Sometimes the flow along a particular sidewalk is pretty much in one direction; sometimes two flows in opposite directions separate themselves on different sides of the sidewalk; at still other times the flow is chaotically intermingled.

This flow of humanity is not constant; it stops and starts. From your high vantage point, the flow of humanity seems to "clot" from time to time, and then the clots dissolve. People stop at an intersection and wait for the light to change, or they simply pause to let a passing car go by. Another clot of humanity awaits the cross-campus bus. Still more clots appear at the cafeteria, the bookstore, and so forth.

Now in place of seeing a flow of particles, I want you to "see" something quite different in these imaginary scenes. See the relationships that exist between and among those hurrying particles. Two people approach each other on the sidewalk. They look up, make eye contact, maybe even nod and say hello. Each moves a little to his or her right so that they can pass by without bumping into each other.

Imagine yourself as one of those people. Imagine you are on your way to the library when you bump into a classmate you know slightly but would like to know better. You say hello and, on the pretense of asking about a class assignment, you strike up an extended conversation.

Notice how your experience of that interaction, as well as your behavior in it, was shaped by the characteristics of the other person, in comparison with your own. Whether you were of the same or a different gender would have affected the nature of your brief encounter, as would your relative ages. How you behaved toward each other—including the possibility of avoiding eye contact and seeming to ignore each other— would have been affected by how the two of you were dressed. (Imagine what the interaction would have been like if the other person was *naked!*)

The nature of your passing interaction would have been similarly affected by the person's race or ethnicity, length and style of hair, the way she or he walked, what she or he was carrying, and so forth. And each of these would depend on your own qualities in each of these respects. Add to this, finally, that the nature of the interaction would unfold with each of your actions conditioning the actions of the other. If you nod and say hello, for example, that would greatly increase the likelihood of the other person doing the same.

Now that you have a sense of the complexity involved in two individuals meeting by chance on a campus sidewalk, multiply that by all of the other pairings that are occurring simultaneously. Not only are you experiencing a series of such encounters as you walk along your way, but also hundreds and thousands of other people are experiencing tens and hundreds of thousands of similar encounters. (You also are engaged in what is called *microsociology,* using a *symbolic interactionist paradigm.*)

It may be useful to imagine lines connecting each pair of interacting humans. See the lines getting shorter and then longer as the individuals approach and then pass by each other. Try to imbue each of those imaginary lines with all of the qualities of the experiences people have in those interactions and the characteristics that shape those experiences.

Now recognize that the relationships we've been imagining are not limited to couples: Sometimes three or more people participate in the same encounter. Everything I've said above still holds but is multiplied in complexity. Consider all of the possible variations in the age, gender, and ethnic makeup of a gathering of three people. Notice that the way A interacts with B is affected not only by A's and B's characteristics but also by C's as well. Imagine, for example, the conversation you'd have with your true love in the presence of (a) your best friend, compared to the conversation you'd have in the presence of (b) your mother, (c) your professor, (d) someone you were considering as a replacement for your current love, or (e) someone you sensed your true love was considering as a replacement for you.

It's a fascinating exercise, trying to observe the passing flow of life in this fashion, trying to perceive all of the imaginary lines connecting individuals as they come into and move out of each other's lives. And it's vastly more interesting and certainly more challenging to observe your own life in this fashion.

It's worth taking this exercise seriously. You might take a moment right now to look around you and observe people in the manner I have been describing. Wherever you are now, if people are around you—in a library or a cafeteria, for example—try to see the imaginary lines of relationships connecting the individuals moving around you. Notice especially what it's like when you are brought into the action as a participant. If you are not around people right now, try to recall the last time you were around people and reconstruct that episode in your mind as I've suggested.

If you are successful in this exercise, you will have had an experience similar to what physicists sometimes have when they reflect that the page they are reading is actually a constant flow of electrons, protons, and other atomic particles in an ever-changing set of relationships to one another. It is akin to the experience a biologist sometimes has in looking at a grandparent, parent, and child and "seeing" the survival of a gene pool across generations.

What you have experienced in the exercise I've suggested is actually more sophisticated than the experience of the physicist and the biologist, however. For their experiences to be comparable to yours, the physicist would have to see his or her hands as being composed of ever-moving atomic particles or, more to the point, to recognize that the brain that played host to such reflections was itself a mass of hurrying electrons and protons: atomic particles thinking about atomic particles. By the same token, the biologist would need to reflect on whether the *idea* of gene pools perpetuating themselves was the product of such survival mechanisms.

Sociological inquiry has a *recursive* quality that is not common in physics or biology: Our inquiries double-back on themselves. Sociologists study human behavior, and what we learn about human behavior affects how we behave, possibly altering what we just learned. Moreover, our inquiries even extend to *how* we learn about ourselves, and insights in that realm can change the way we look for new insights, not to mention what the subsequent inquiries reveal. If you take a moment to think about how you are thinking or try to look directly at the back of your head, you should gain some appreciation for the complexity that recursiveness adds to social inquiry.

The recursive nature of humans studying what it means to be human is one of two features that make sociology the most fascinating and challenging of sciences. The second feature is that many of our social creations can achieve an unanticipated and unintended *permanence;* sometimes they seem to take on lives of their own. Let's look at some examples of that.

Earlier I asked you to notice how the flow of humanity was marked by frequent "clotting." Couples and small groups come together and persist for a time. Two friends may stop for a conversation. Strangers may gather momentarily to watch a street preacher, a traffic accident, or an Elvis impersonator in a passing limousine.

When strangers form such chance groupings, they often interact and thereby establish relationships deeper than passing encounters. They talk to other individuals and to the group at large:

"This guy should be on TV."

"I think the red car was to blame."

"I guess Elvis moved out of Minneapolis."

Depending on what brought them together, the little clots of humanity may persist for less than a minute, for several minutes, or even longer. Then the clots dissolve.

Some gatherings have more form and persistence, however. Imagine a stadium filled with 70,000 screaming football fans. Most of them do not know each other and might not even care to. And yet they have all come together at the same location for roughly the same purpose. Take a moment to visualize the lines of relationships connecting individuals throughout that mass of 70,000. For 3 or 4 hours, they will constitute a shifting mass of relationships among themselves. At times, they will operate more or less in concert. They will rise in relative silence and solemnity as a popular rock star sings the national anthem, adding interpretations never anticipated by Francis Scott Key. From time to time, the fans will join in the "wave" sweeping around the stadium.

Sometimes the relationships will not be altogether cooperative or coordinated. Fights may break out between fans of the opposing sides. People may shout at each other and throw things. (Sociologists refer to this phenomenon as *collective behavior*.) Notice, however, that these kinds of interactions represent relationships as much as cordial conversations among friends. Notice as well that the course of a fistfight will be conditioned by the characteristics of the participants and of those among whom they have staged their fight.

There is a certain magic about being a part of a mass audience like that assembled for a football game. Something similar can be said for those gathered for an evening at the symphony or the opera, though there are usually fewer fistfights and the wave is, I believe, against the law. Still, something happens among the hundreds or thousands of people gathered together for Puccini's *Madama Butterfly*. There is a strong sense that they are no longer individuals as they live through Cho-cho-san's soaring love for Pinkerton, her devotion in his long absence, and her despair and death due to his betrayal. Those gathered in the audience have become something more than a mere collection of individuals. Although it's difficult to say what exactly has been created, you need only be there to know that it has happened.

And then everyone goes home. After the game is over, the fans pick up their belongings and file out to the parking lot by way of the toilets and start the drive home. The opera-goers do the same, though they seem less in need of the restrooms (there are no "toilets" at the opera).

Everyone goes home, and the particular gatherings we've just witnessed will never come together again. A mass of individuals came together and created something bigger than the sum of their individualities; it persisted for a while; and then it was gone forever. A vast proportion of human social life is of this nature.

But sometimes the special something we create together *persists*. In 1789, a group of white men came together to form something called the United States Senate. More than 200 years later, that Senate still exists. None of the original members are still alive. In fact, hundreds of members have passed through the Senate during its 2 centuries of existence, and yet somehow we feel that *the Senate itself has persisted*.

In 1636, a young American colonist named John Harvard gave $2,000 and some books for the establishment of the first college in the New World. More than 350 years later, Harvard College persists. Although virtually everything about it has changed—size, students, faculty, library, and so on—we still have the sense that something that we call Harvard has survived the centuries.

Some organizations are very short-lived. Sometimes we try to form a club, call a first meeting, no one comes, and we give up the idea. It's not clear whether the organization ever existed at all except in our minds. Some organizations are created formally, last for a time, fade, and disappear. Restaurants, for example, are a risky business venture, showing a tendency to change into video rental outlets. Some organizations can last for a fairly long time before changing circumstances or dramatic events drive them into extinction; consider the Union of Soviet Socialist Republics, for example. And then, some organizations seem to last forever. Harvard's not a bad example, but notice that the Roman Catholic Church has Harvard beaten by more than 15 centuries.

THE CONCEPT OF SOCIAL STRUCTURE

This investigation is not limited to organizations per se. Organizations belong to a more general category: social structure. Examples of social structure include relationship patterns among individuals, small groups, formal organizations, institutions, and whole social systems, as well as beliefs, values, norms, sanctions, and many other phenomena. The concept of *social structure* is an acknowledgement that human social behavior is not random: It follows certain patterns that can be discovered and understood. Something as mundane as the daily congestion of morning commute traffic is an example of social structure. So is the fact that all of the cars are traveling on the right-hand side of the road. The fact that the cars in New Zealand would be traveling on the left-hand side of the road is an element of that society's social structure.

All laws and customs are examples of social structure. All established patterns of behavior are also social structure. This is an investigation, therefore, of persistent patterns in human social life. We want to find out why some patterns persist and others do not. To find the answer to this question, however, we must take a view of social structure slightly different from that we've been doing.

What we call social structure is not really a structure at all; it is a *process*. It is a structural or organizational process. More specifically, *social structure* is a process of taking away individual freedom and structuring it for corporate action.

A university, for example, is an ongoing process in which students and faculty give up possibilities for action so that they can come together for a limited set of interactions. I give up the freedom to lecture on brain surgery, not to mention the freedom to watch daytime TV, and agree to come into the classroom and talk about social science research methods. A number of students give up their own sets of possibilities to join me in that classroom.

Social structure is a dynamic process in which the agreements to give up freedoms and the remaining possibilities for action are always in flux. Thus, when sociologists set out to discover the structure of society, they are, in a sense, doomed to failure in that quest because society isn't structured: it is a *process* of structuring. *Society is a self-structuring, self-organizing, self-creating process.*

Notice, for example, that every session of Congress is devoted to changing the structure of the government. Tax systems are changed. New agencies are created; others are expanded; occasionally agencies are shut down. Typically we witness a negotiation between the agenda of the president and the Congress. If you reflect on it for a moment, you'll see that the operation of our federal government is one of restructuring itself.

Now let's shift to a very different example. English is the predominant language of the United States. Yet our use of the language is constantly changing. Some of the changes originate in technology: *meltdown, feedback loop, going ballistic.* Many of the changes originate with the young: the cat's meow, heavy, groovy. (I've purposely chosen very dated examples because any current ones may very well be dated by the time you read this.) Thus we constantly are changing the structure of our communications and doing it within the context of communicating.

From time to time, the news media enjoy presenting articles on "what's in" and "what's out." If you've seen more than one such article over time, you've recognized that fads and foibles come and go. As soon as you've filled your closet with the latest fashions, you discover they've gone out of style.

Thus sociologists are devoted to studying something that won't stand still. It is constantly changing. As I've suggested above, society is more a process of structuring than a fixed structure.

Add the recursive quality, and our quest becomes all the more complex when we realize that we cannot study society from anywhere other than the eye of the storm. There is an advantage, of course, in that such a vantage point brings us close to the action, but the disadvantage is that while we try to study the self-structuring process that is society, the same process is structuring our search—including the ways you and I think.

When Karl Marx (1875) wrote of the "class struggle" in human history, he did much more than observe something about the state of human affairs. His writings produced many attempts to alter the nature of that struggle. Some reformers and revolutionaries, for example, sought to make workers more conscious of their class identity and interests, thus recognizing the oppression they suffered and organizing themselves to overcome it. The actions of the working class obviously altered the nature of the class struggle Marx had written about. Because the workers' actions also affected the behavior of the capitalists, the struggle was altered even further.

The organization of workers in some countries, such as the United States, led to the development of powerful labor unions, which were able to bargain with owners and management for improved working conditions and worker compensation. The organized labor movement so radically altered the nature of the class struggle as originally described that Marx himself finally commented that a class revolution might be unnecessary in such situations (Lipset, 1963).

Consider, for example, the notion of *cybernetics:* automatic communication and control systems involving "feedback loops" and "servo-mechanisms." A simple illustration of this notion is found in most home heating systems. The thermostat (a servo-mechanism) monitors the room temperature. Whenever the temperature drops too low, the thermostat sends a signal (feedback) to the furnace, turning it on. When the temperature rises to a specified level, the thermostat sends another signal, turning the furnace off. Most of the scientific discussion of cybernetics has focused on computers. Antilock brakes on modern automobiles are a good example of computer cybernetics put to practical use.

At the same time, sociologists of organizations have recognized that this concept also can be applied to human behavior. And the more we have become "aware" of cybernetics in social affairs, the more consciously we have built cybernetic mechanisms into those affairs. Now organizational consultants lecture managers on the importance of structuring feedback loops through which the flow of information continues to inform appropriate action. And, of course, if the information flow indicates that the flow of information itself is faulty, the appropriate action is to establish more effective feedback loops. The circularity of such matters can be dizzying to comprehend.

These latest comments point to the most challenging aspect of the sociologist's study of society: *Whatever we learn about the way society is organizing itself, that knowledge will affect the process we have just discovered.* Thus the process we've just discovered will no longer exist in its just-discovered form. Sociology is a continuing process of "mis-covery." Although we can learn things about society, we alter them in the process of learning about them.

Consider this example of what I'm talking about. Currently the notion of *co-dependency* is a popular one in social psychology, and co-dependent relationships are being identified every day. In the case of alcoholism, for example, it is easy to see ways the alcoholic in a family becomes dependent on others. Less obvious are the ways the others in the family can become dependent on the alcoholic member. The alcoholic is someone others can feel morally superior to, someone to focus "mothering instincts" on, and so forth.

As we have come to understand the extent to which such relationships serve the needs of all involved, it has become apparent that merely curing the defects of one member won't work. Recognizing that you are in a co-dependent relationship with someone, however, is likely to alter that relationship.

Because every relationship is actually a process for structuring your interactions with another, the nature of that structuring process is altered. Even if you do not give up all elements of co-dependency, the relationship simply will not continue to function exactly as it did before. So from inside a relationship, we learn something about its nature, and what we learn causes the relationship to alter, thereby making what we learned no longer accurate.

Here's a very different example of recursiveness in human affairs, as we move from co-dependent families to the stock market. As the stock market has become more complex, traders have discovered momentary opportunities for surefire profits in what is known as *arbitrage.*

The stock market consists primarily of the matching of buying and selling prices of specific stocks. If the selling price of a stock is higher than the buying price, no sales occur. As soon as selling prices drop to what buyers are willing to pay or when buying prices rise to reach what sellers are willing to accept, then sales take place. Sometimes in the flux and flow of a complex market, however, some sellers are willing to sell stocks for less than others are willing to pay, each being unaware of the other. The trader who can discover such disparities can make a quick and sure profit: buying low and selling high.

As traders have grown more aware of such possibilities, special effort has been devoted to finding ways of discovering arbitrage opportunities swiftly. Because nothing can process masses of data more swiftly than computers, we should not be surprised to find the development of arbitrage computer programs. Nor should we be surprised to find their use proliferating among stock market traders.

Many observers of Wall Street believe that programmed trading played a central role in nearly destroying the stock market and the American economy with it a few years ago. The culprit was its recursiveness.

On October 19, 1987, the recursive potential of this situation came to a head. Arbitrage programs told traders to begin buying and selling according to specific patterns. As many of them did so, however, the situation changed radically, causing the programs to respond with new instructions for action. Now, suddenly, trading shifted directions, changing the state of the market once more, producing new programmed trading instructions. This unfolding process was accompanied with a growing panic among the hapless humans involved. By the end of the day, the Dow Jones average had dropped more than 500 points: a loss of 22.6%. Although it is difficult to estimate such things, the value of stocks on the several major stock exchanges may have plunged by nearly $1 trillion.

Once again, we see an example of a human social creation taking on a life of its own—its recursive quality, in this case, being abetted by computers. Not all cases of this phenomenon are as dramatic as the 1987 stock market crash, but many other examples have a far greater impact on your life. We will examine how they do that.

CONCLUSION

In this chapter, you've gotten an initial glimpse of the strange phenomenon that concerns this book: *social structure*. We've seen that although human beings create the patterns that govern their lives, those patterns can take on lives of their own, slipping out of human control. In this initial discussion, you've previewed most of the topics that concern the remainder of this book.

Certainly sociologists study a phenomenon no less strange than the quarks, black holes, and big bangs that have captured the fancy of physicists. In contrast to the physicist's black hole, however, there is a possibility of humans regaining control of society.

In sum, sociologists study an invisible world of entities that we ourselves create but that often come to control us. We cannot study those entities except from within the shadow of their control, and whatever we learn about them will alter them at least slightly, thereby making the recovery of control that much more elusive.

In Chapter 2, we look more closely into the *reality* of this strange phenomenon. Even though social structure is intangible, it has a powerful effect on your life.

Points of Discussion

- State some examples of your creating or being present at the creation of social structure.

- I've said that social structure is invisible. Still, physical traces of social structure are all around us. What are some examples of those traces?

- Recall the discussion of the evolution of The Holiday Project. In what ways might the Board of Directors have reduced the extent to which organizational concerns grew in importance?

Reading Further

If you'd like to augment your introduction to sociology, you might enjoy *The Sociological Spirit* (Belmont, CA: Wadsworth, 1988), a small book in which I attempted to cover the main concepts and perspectives of this exciting field of inquiry. Or you might enjoy the somewhat older, but still fascinating, book I modeled *Spirit* after: Peter Berger's *Invitation to Sociology* (Garden City, NY: Doubleday, 1963).

Another classic by Peter Berger (with co-author Thomas Luckman), *The Social Construction of Reality* (Garden City, NY: Doubleday, 1966), offers a powerful and readable discussion of how we humans create our environment. This is a fundamental point that we pursue in this book, and I know it can be a difficult one to grasp because it challenges our conventional notions of objectivity and reality.

Finally, you may be ready to plunge into the sociological study of organizations. If so, I recommend Gareth Morgan's *Images of Organizations* (Beverly Hills, CA: Sage, 1986), which is organized around the various metaphors that have been used for understanding organizations: organizations as machines, as organisms, and so on.

CHAPTER TWO

Social Structure Is Real

Social structure exists. It is created by human beings, but then it takes on a life of its own. Once established as a self-sustaining entity, social structure becomes a powerful force in determining the lives of those who created it.

In 1953, science fiction master Theodore Sturgeon published his finest novel, *More Than Human*. In it, he relates the experiences of a group of five rather unusual human beings. Janie is a little girl who has suffered a great deal of neglect and lacks the experience of love, but she also possesses adult intelligence plus the powers of telepathy (reading minds) and telekinesis (moving objects with the power of her mind).

Bonnie and Beanie are twin sisters who have the power of teleportation: They can transport themselves anywhere instantly. Gerry is an angry young delinquent who literally can steal people's thoughts and can force the people to do his will by getting them to look into his eyes.

The group is completed by a Down syndrome baby whose rapidly expanding brain is capable of receiving and analyzing vast amounts of data in a manner that would rival the most powerful computers.

Although not one of the five is suitable for survival as an individual, their various strengths and weaknesses blend and mesh together (Sturgeon said they "blesh") to form something awesome. Sturgeon called it a *homo gestalt*, which he suggested was an evolutionary jump. Put together, the young misfits formed something truly "more than human."

As I've thought about it over the years, I've come to realize that I have been living as part of a homo gestalt all my life. That's what society is; so are all of the smaller organizations we create to get specific jobs done. This book is about the nature of homo gestalt and how it turns on us.

This is a fundamental principle of sociology: *Human groups are more than collections of human beings*. When people come together to make a common cause, they create something special; they become something that did not exist before then.

One of the founders of sociology, Emile Durkheim (1897/1951), said society existed *sui generis*, meaning that it could not be reduced to smaller elements. It had an existence that was beyond the parts that comprised it.

Perhaps this was the intent of the New Testament passage in which Jesus said, "Wherever two or three are gathered together in my name, there, too, am I." He seems to have been saying that whenever Christians gathered together as Christians, something was created that existed beyond the specific individuals so gathered.

Although his aims were quite different, Adolf Hitler had the same process in mind when he stirred the German masses to establish a political being that would outlast all of those who were present at its birth. In that spirit, he proclaimed the foundation of a "thousand-year Reich." Germany's defeat in World War II seemed to block his intent, though the periodic resurgence of neo-Nazism may suggest that Hitler was more successful than we are aware.

Clearly the "something else" that humans sometimes create when they come together can work for good or for evil, but it is, in any event, a very powerful phenomenon. This book is devoted to an understanding of that special entity, and before we are finished, you may find that you've begun to feel some sympathy for Dr. Jekyll and/or Mr. Hyde.

THE REALITY OF SOCIAL STRUCTURE

Ask sociology professors around the country what their most difficult task is, and many will tell you that it involves getting students to grasp the existence, the reality, of *social structure*. In general, this term refers to the great many patterns we develop for relating to one another and organizing our relationships in society.

As I indicated in Chapter 1, sociologists use the term *social structure* in reference to a fairly broad range of phenomena: informal social groups, formal organizations, whole societies, and other collective forms that human beings organize themselves into. It includes all of the rules we establish for living together: our governments, religions, systems of morality, codes of etiquette, and the like. The organization of a military battalion, comprised of companies, platoons, squads, and individual soldiers, is a clear example of social structure. So is the organization of workers, supervisors, and managers in a factory. The traditional relationships between men and women in a society, between young and old, and among religious, racial, and ethnic groups are all examples of social structure. A democratic political system with elected officials, appointed bureaucrats, taxes, and so forth is another example of social structure. So is a system of totalitarian dictatorship.

The bedrock assumption of this analysis is that forms of social structure (organizations, institutions, societies, etc.) are entities separate from human individuals. Even though you cannot, as a practical matter, have an organization without individual humans, there is a very important sense in which organizations exist separate from those individuals.

Physicists speak of a *quantum* difference in this sense. For example, we cannot learn enough about iron (e.g., it's hard, dense, attracted to magnets, etc.) to understand the iron atom or atomic structure in general. Submolecular processes operate on a different level, according to different rules, from iron as an element. Looking in a different direction, conceptually, we cannot learn enough about iron to understand the sociology of the Iron Age.

By the same token, you cannot learn enough about human beings to understand human groups. Here's a different analogy to illustrate what I mean by the existence of social structure and its separateness from human beings.

Imagine four people standing in the four corners of a room. Notice that their positions represent a rectangle. If you drew lines along the baseboards to connect the four people, those lines would represent a rectangle. Notice the sense in which the four people form a rectangle. The rectangle exists.

In addition, you can draw a line connecting two opposing corners, and you will have formed two right triangles. We could say, in fact, that any three of the four people are forming a right triangle.

It is important to recognize that although the rectangle and the triangles we've been discussing are formed by human beings, nothing we know about humans tells us anything about the geometric forms. For example, we can determine the genders of the four people forming the rectangle, but it makes no sense to ask the gender of the rectangle itself. It is not just that the rectangle is neither male nor female, but more that the question does not even apply. The notion of gender is alien to the nature of the rectangle. By the same token, it makes no sense even to consider whether the rectangle is Democratic or Republican, Protestant or Catholic, rich or poor, educated or uneducated, and so forth.

None of the foregoing should suggest to us that rectangles and triangles are somehow unknowable. We have learned all sorts of things about geometric forms, some of which you may even remember from high school. You can determine the area of a rectangle by multiplying its length times its width, for example. The area of any of the right triangles is half of that. The length of the hypotenuse connecting the opposing corners of the rectangle is equal to the square root of the sum of the squares of the two legs. In fact, we could state this as something we know about rectangles: the distance between opposing corners.

Far from being mysterious and unknowable, the forms we study in Euclidian geometry have a reassuring consistency, certainty, and clarity. They are eminently understandable, and we understand a lot about them. However, things we have learned about human beings—what causes prejudice, how education affects income, religious differences of men and women—none of this assists us in understanding the rectangles and triangles that human beings may from time to time choose to form.

Notice that the mismatch of concepts to entity goes in the other direction as well. Imagine yourself to be one of the humans creating the rectangle and triangles. What is the length of your hypotenuse? The sum of the angles in the rectangle is 360°; how about yours?

The point of this tortured review of plain geometry is that although the rectangle and the triangles in our example are formed by individual human beings, we cannot learn enough about humans to understand rectangles and triangles. The same is true of the relationships, groups, organizations, institutions, and societies that human beings form. Although it is possible to learn about the nature of organizations, it is quite different from the nature of human beings.

For now, let's examine some of the elements of social structure that illustrate the reality I've been arguing for.

SOME ELEMENTS AND FORMS OF SOCIAL STRUCTURE

Relationships

Perhaps the most basic form of social structure that you can recognize in your own experience is the *social relationship*. You experience many relationships in your life. First, you are the child of some mother and father, and most of us grow up with those two relationships being of special importance. In fact, if you were orphaned in infancy, you are likely to be powerfully influenced by the *lack* of those relationships.

Let's begin with some of the elements of social structure to be found in social relationships. Then we'll consider larger and more complex forms of social structure.

If you have siblings, the relationships you form with those brothers and/or sisters will be important ones for you. The relationships you form with other relatives may be equally important to you. What does it mean to say that such relationships are "important"? On the one hand, they provide for a variety of your psychological needs: security, a sense of belonging and feeling loved. In your early years, of course, the relationships you have with family members allow you to *live*. But these relationships are important in another way, one that is more germane to our present inquiry. Social relationships offer you a *blueprint for behavior*.

At some point in your life, your mother told you what to eat and you ate it, what clothes to wear and you wore them. Maybe she still does. As you grew up, you learned there were some things you could say to your mother and other things you could not. We can define your relationship with your mother, let's say, as that set of patterns you have for interacting with one another. Some general similarities can be found in such relationships within a given culture, and every mother-child relationship is also unique in certain ways. If you have siblings, for example, your mother has a somewhat different relationship with each of her children.

Other social relationships in your life might include friendship relationships, love relationships, and marital relationships. You have experienced a number of student-teacher relationships. You may have experienced the relationships that exist between workers and employers. Drive too fast, and you'll experience the relationship that exists between police officers and the driving public. Drive really fast, and you'll develop a relationship with judges and attorneys. And if you are really, really bad, your collection could extent to include bail-bond agents, jurors, and even wardens, guards, and fellow prisoners.

Each of these relationships differs from the others in that a different set of expectations pertains to your behavior in dealing with the various partners in those relationships. If you are accustomed to calling your best friend by the nickname Grizzly Dude and to greeting him or her with a poke in the arm or other body part, do not attempt that behavior with the police officer who wants to see your driver's license or the judge who wants to see whether you are sorry for being bad.

Notice that your social relationships are *real*. You are really expected to behave in certain ways with certain people, and other forms of behavior definitely would be out of line. The wrong behavior can get you yelled at, shut out, or dead. That's how real social structure is.

Now let's look at some of the distinctions sociologists make among the various aspects of social structure that we've been previewing.

Status

In discussing some of your social relationships, I made reference to a variety of partners in those relationships. Sociologists use the term *social status* in that regard. A social status is a location within a relationship. In the mother-son relationship, both "mother" and "son" are social statuses.

Other common social statuses include father, daughter, friend, teacher, TV salesperson, home improvement show host, hardware store clerk, 911 operator, and ambulance driver. All kinship positions are statuses; so are all occupations. Voter is a status, as is politician, campaign manager, precinct worker, and so forth. Democrat, Republican, and Independent are statuses. So are Protestant, Catholic, Jew, Hindu, Moslem, Buddhist, and atheist.

It is sometimes useful to see certain personal orientations as social statuses: Conservative person and liberal person are examples. Honest person and thief might be usefully seen as social statuses. The term can be applied usefully in any situation where there may be expectations regarding interactions between such people. Thus, for example, two liberals would have a different conversation than we would expect between a liberal and a conservative.

It is worth noting, in passing, how statuses must exist in sets. You cannot have liberals, for example, without the possibility of conservatives. The status "man" has no meaning without the status "woman." We cannot have old people without young people.

Roles

Sociologists have a technical term for the "expectations" associated with statuses: *roles*. The term was introduced by anthropologist Ralph Linton in 1936. He distinguished statuses and roles as follows:

> A status, as distinct from the individual who may occupy it, is simply a collection of rights and duties. . . . A role represents the dynamic aspect of a status. The individual is socially assigned to a status and occupies it with relation to other statuses. When he puts the rights and duties which constitute the status into effect, he is performing a role. (Linton, 1936, p. 114)

Roles, then, are a critical part of social structure. Notice how "real" the roles you occupy are. Although some of the expectations you feel are perhaps rather casual, many are not. I cannot guess which are the most significant for you, of course. Some people, however, are particularly serious about pleasing their parents. Parents tend to take the protection of their young children pretty seriously.

Students are expected to answer their own exams and not to look at the answers being written by neighboring classmates. As an American citizen, you are expected to refrain from selling state secrets to other nations (in case you've been grappling with that option). Your banker is expected to leave your money in the bank and not take it out for a wild weekend in Acapulco. If you are married, you probably are expected to limit your sexual expression.

Role expectations like these tend to be taken pretty seriously. Even though you cannot "see" the expectations and many are not even written down, they are very real.

Norms and Sanctions

Sociologists use the term *norm* to refer to expectations that apply broadly within a society but are not linked to specific social statuses. In many cases, the terms *norm* and *role* are used almost interchangeably.

Some norms are codified in laws. Thus we have norms that prohibit murder, theft, rape, arson, and so forth. Less dramatic norms tell us where we can or cannot park, for how long, and at what cost. Other norms tell us which side of the road to drive on and how fast. Norms like these are also very real—as real as the jail you can live in if you doubt the reality of these elements of social structure.

Other norms are more informal but very real all the same. When you are introduced to someone, the person probably will say hello and extend a hand to you. You will be expected to say hello and to shake that hand. Stick your tongue out instead, and you'll learn another lesson about the reality of the norms comprising our social structure. Do it once, and people may think you a little odd; do it regularly, and you may get sent off to live with other people who do that.

Some norms you can probably violate without being institutionalized. You can be really obese and never get locked up for it. However, you may have trouble getting dates and getting certain jobs, and you may find yourself excluded from numerous other activities. People may snicker at you and even make rude remarks. (Obese persons seem to be the last minority group that it's acceptable to be prejudiced against and to make fun of; there seem to be norms *against* such behaviors applied to other minority groups.)

In general, abiding by the norms of your society will bring rewards; violating them will result in punishments. Sociologists call these *positive sanctions* and *negative sanctions*, respectively. Both positive and negative sanctions can vary in intensity, but they are real.

Values

Often the norms we are brought up to respect and obey are justified in terms of more general values. Thus the norm prohibiting murder is based on the value we place on human life. The prohibition against theft is based on the value of private property.

Sometimes the relationship between norms and values is not obvious or direct. Sometimes norms are justified in terms of maintaining public order or decorum.

Values are another element of social structure, and they are as real as any of the other elements. Denying their reality can be as dangerous as denying the reality of the garbage truck bearing down on your new convertible.

Our discussion of the elements of social structure already has begun to take us beyond simple relationships, so let's turn directly now to other, more complex forms of social structure.

Groups

Groups are a somewhat more complex form of social structure than a simple relationship. Although this term is used somewhat flexibly, sociologists distinguish groups from simple gatherings or aggregations of people. Generally we reserve the term *group* for entities that have a lasting identity and some degree of organization. Your family would qualify as a social group. So would a clique or gang you regularly hang around with. A sorority or fraternity, the sociology department faculty at a college, a Marine Corps platoon, your high school graduating class, the U.S. Senate: All are examples of social groups.

Note that each of these examples has a determinate membership and that the participants in each group recognize themselves as members. In fact, membership in the group constitutes a part of members' sense of who they are. Moreover, the members of such groups usually have different expectations about each other's behavior in the group; this is what I meant by "some degree of organization." There are differing expectations for the different members of a family, for example. In the

U.S. Senate, some are senior members, some junior; there are committee chairs, and so forth. In some groups, such as friendship cliques, the expectations of different members are informal, representing patterns of interaction that have evolved over time.

Groups are as real as other forms of social structure. Some are written into law. Others exhibit their reality in the interactions of members over time. If you habitually meet for coffee with a group of friends every Monday morning at 10:00, try skipping next week and see whether that informal group really exists or not. Chances are, the other members will want an accounting for your absence. Or if you are the one who always makes the coffee, don't do it next Monday; notice how real that role is for everyone else. (And notice how cranky they are without their coffee.)

Formal Organizations

Formal organizations represent a special kind of group. Although definitions vary, organizations differ from other groups by being deliberately formed and by having a more explicit structure. Thus the U.S. Senate is more of a formal organization than your family, despite how senators sometimes behave on television. General Motors, Ford, and Chrysler are all formal organizations. So are the Boy Scouts of America and the Roman Catholic Church. McDonald's, Disneyland, and Yale University are formal organizations too.

Traditionally sociologists have added that formal organizations are constituted for the purpose of pursuing some goal, such as GM building cars. Whether and to what extent organizations really are based on accomplishing goals is a major issue for us to examine in this book. It may turn out, for example, that organizations are pursuing goals, but not the goals their participants have in mind.

INSTITUTIONALIZATION AND INSTITUTIONS

I began this discussion of the elements and forms of social structure by discussing relationships and the patterns of interaction we form. This formation is true when you and a friend develop certain patterns of being with one another, and it is true when your friendship clique falls into a pattern of meeting for coffee every Monday morning at 10:00. Sociologists refer to the establishment and perpetuation of social patterns as the process of *institutionalization*. Institutionalization also occurs on a grander scale. Societies evolve patterns of social relationships. Consider family relations in American society.

European settlers to the New World brought with them a pattern of monogamous marriage (one husband, one wife), in contrast to some other societies that practice *polygamy*, wherein a husband may have more than one wife (*polygyny*) or a wife may have more than one husband (*polyandry*). In contrast to the extended families of Europe (several generations living together in one household), Americans established a norm of the nuclear family (married couple and their children). And in contrast to societies where families are dominated by the husband/ father (*patriarchal*) or by the wife/mother (*matriarchal*), the norm in modern America is the egalitarian family in which power is shared.

It is important to realize that in all of these examples, I am talking about overall normative patterns of American society—and none of them are universal patterns in practice. Certainly some marriages are totally dominated by the wife, for example, and some are totally dominated by the husband. The reality of the overall norm, however, is seen in the fact that most Americans would describe such marriages as unusual, inappropriate, or dysfunctional, depending on how strongly they felt about the matter.

The sociological term *institution* is used fairly casually in everyday conversation, with some differing meanings. Sometimes banks are referred to as financial institutions, and loyal alumni sometimes speak respectfully of Harvard as an institution. In both cases, the term *organization* would be more appropriate.

In sociological usage, the term *institution* is reserved for the system of institutionalized norms and values, roles and statuses that generally organize relations within some broad sector of social life. The five institutions most commonly named by sociologists are religion, education, government, economy, and family. Sometimes it is useful to focus on more somewhat specific portions of social life. Sometimes we speak of the labor movement, the military, higher education, or Roman Catholicism as institutions. To the extent that we are interested in discovering established patterns of norms, values, roles, and statuses, that usage is appropriate.

The relationship between organizations and institutions is a useful one to note briefly. Organizations operate within the constraints represented by institutional patterns. General Motors, for example, is an organization that must function within the patterns comprising the American economy: basically capitalist, though with government regulations, an active labor union, and so forth. One implication of this relationship is that more powerful social change often can be rendered by focusing on institutional norms rather than on specific individuals or organizations.

Early in his career in public advocacy, Ralph Nader had a specific concern regarding a specific automobile he believed to be unsafe. Eventually, however, he shifted his concern to regulations affecting all auto manufacturers. His greater impact, however, was in the establishment of *consumer rights* as a general concept. Thus he brought about significant changes in the institutions of government and economy, thereby affecting the behavior of countless organizations and individuals.

Like the other elements of social structure, institutions are very real. They have enormous power over your life.

CULTURE

The elements of social structure shared by some groups are generally referred to as its *culture*. I'm sure you know of some small group that could be described in terms of its culture. Perhaps you know of a club, a gang, or a friendship clique that generally is known to others for certain persistent characteristics. On a college campus, some fraternities are known as "jock fraternities" in reference to their predominant membership and behavioral patterns. Some sororities are known as predominantly oriented to social life, pep rallies, and the like. Others are known as havens of serious intellectual scholars.

Go into any small to mid-sized town in America, and you are likely to find people who can tell you about the differences separating the Lions, the Rotary, and the Kiwanis social service clubs. You'll also be able to learn that the local Baptist, Episcopal, and Lutheran congregations differ in many ways other than their religious beliefs.

Culture is real. It exists. It is in this sense that we can speak legitimately about "The Jewish People" or the "The Arabs" as meaning something more than the human beings currently occupying the statuses named by those terms. A group's culture persists far longer than any of the humans who have shared in it.

SOCIETY AS AN ORGANISM

A great many social thinkers have taken the view that society could be seen usefully as an organism or a distinct entity. Auguste Comte, who coined the term *sociologie*, established this point of view at the dawning of the discipline. In more recent years, this way of seeing society has been known as *functionalism* or *social systems theory*. The basic premise is that society is a system composed of numerous component parts, each of which plays its role in the functioning of the whole.

The functionalist view can be applied to smaller scale phenomena. A football team offers an excellent example of this view: The quarterback has his job to do, and so do the running backs, the tight ends, and so on. Or, if you prefer, a symphony orchestra offers an equally good illustration, with the conductor, strings, horns, percussion, and so on. In both cases, the whole is truly greater than the sum of its parts.

In the social systems view, every part of society—by virtue of its existence—must serve some function. This assertion holds even for those aspects of society we regard as problematic. Crime, for example, serves functions. It keeps the police employed, for one thing. Emile Durkheim (1897) also suggested that crime served the function of reminding us of what was acceptable and unacceptable and of the punishments that lay in store whenever we strayed.

Prejudice and injustice can be seen in terms of the functions they serve in society. Herbert Gans (1971) has drawn our attention to some of the functions served by poverty—for example, a work force willing to do "dirty jobs," a market for imperfect goods, an incentive for others to be successful, and job opportunities for social workers. None of this analysis should be used to justify poverty but only to show how it fits into the rest of society. Indeed, if you wanted to end poverty, it would be important to know what other parts of society would be affected. It may be necessary to find other ways of serving the functions currently served by poverty.

The social systems view is a useful one, and it has predominated American sociology for most of the latter half of this century. It has enjoyed less favor in recent years, however, on the assumption that stating the functions of something seemed to justify its existence. Functionalists have been painted as inherently conservative, though I don't think this is a justified complaint.

A more serious problem plagues the functionalist view. Whenever we begin examining human organizations as though they were organisms, there is a strong temptation to start thinking of them as *human*. All too often, we hear people speak of the emotions, personalities, and motivations of organizations. We talk that way in everyday life: "That's what the government wants us to do." "General Motors is afraid you'll like the Toyota." "Germany is more warlike than France."

The social sciences are grounded in the view that human social life is susceptible to rational understanding and explanation. This book makes that same assumption. When we set out to understand organizations, however, we often make the deadly error of assuming that our understanding of human beings will help us understand human organizations. The second principal point of this book is: *Human groups are not human.*

HUMAN GROUPS ARE NOT HUMAN

Human groups do operate according to patterns that can be discovered, understood, and predicted. The logic of those patterns, however, is nothing like the logic that governs the patterns of behavior among human beings.

This is a vital recognition, especially with regard to social problems and attempts at remedial social change. Many of the problems we face as a society are embedded in the structure of social relations rather than in the hearts and minds of individuals. The solutions to those problems also lie in the domain of how we structure our social relations, and the necessary remedies are not the same ones that might be effective with individuals.

Consider the fact that American women still earn only about two-thirds as much as men. This is a long-persistent pattern, and it cannot be explained away on the basis of occupational prestige, hours worked, experience, seniority, or any of the other variables that affect income. If you were to study absolutely matched samples of American men and women, the men would be found to earn substantially more than the women.

Now if we were to discover a particular employer who was systematically underpaying female employees, we'd know what to do. In fact, specific employers are periodically sued for sex discrimination.

In the case of discrimination by individuals, we know how to recognize when it exists, we understand the belief systems and motivations that cause it, and we know some ways of making people stop. We are not equally well equipped to deal with *institutionalized bigotry:* that which is produced by the structure of society itself. It is not produced by the same belief systems and motivations as individual prejudice and discrimination, nor does it respond to the same remedies.

Not long ago, the Supreme Court was asked to declare capital punishment unconstitutional on the grounds that it discriminated against blacks. The plaintiffs offered incontrovertible statistical evidence that blacks were more likely to be executed than whites, even when all other variables (e.g., nature of crime, race and gender of victim) were held constant. Literally "with all else being equal," as in the case of economic discrimination against women, you are simply more likely to be executed in America if you are black than if you are white.

The Supreme Court justices did not dispute the statistical evidence. Still, they did not declare capital punishment unconstitutional on the grounds of racial discrimination. For the disparity in execution rates to be a matter of prejudice, the justices argued, it would be necessary to find individual jurors who would admit having made their decisions on the basis of race. In other words, the justices were unable to conceive of institutionalized discrimination. However, the disparity in execution rates for blacks and whites in America is never going to be solved by dealing with individual jurors who say they made their decisions based on race.

By the same token, when people complain that America is a "racist society," you can be virtually assured that they are thinking of individualized racism even when they speak of institutionalized racism. What most people have in mind is a picture of grown-up bigots passing their bigotry along to the next generation of little bigots-in-waiting. And while that is an accurate picture, it is not all there is to institutionalized racism. It is not even the most important part. And, unfortunately, we don't understand the most important part very well because it doesn't abide by the same logic as human behavior. Human groups are not human.

We will examine the idea of institutional discrimination in greater depth in Chapter 7, but it is an important concept to understand from this point on. Let's look at a few elements in the institutional racism against black Americans.

- The simple fact that blacks earn substantially less than whites at present means that the next generation of black children will have fewer benefits in youth and will have a more meager launching pad into their own adult careers.

- The fact that blacks are more likely to be arrested and prosecuted for crimes creates some level of presumption that any individual black person may be a criminal. Even if today's arrests and prosecutions were all unbiased, the present disparity by race would create biased expectations in the future.

- A mass of jokes stereotyping black people has been passed from generation to generation, and new ones still appear. They form part of a background of negative thoughts about blacks that affect feelings and actions on an unconscious level even when they are explicitly rejected. Some of the jokes portray blacks as inferior to whites; others enforce stereotypes of violence or sexuality that instill some degree of fear.

- The movies, books, and other aspects of culture that perpetuate negative stereotypes about black Americans operate on an unconscious level even when they may be rejected consciously.

- Our most sacred national documents, such as the Constitution, remind us that the founders we deeply revere believed that black people (and Native Americans) were not fully human.

Some of the elements of institutional racism, therefore, are purely structural: Differences in income are the clearest example. Whatever the original source of institutional racism, it has a discriminatory effect regardless of whether or not it affects people's attitudes and feelings. More difficult to recognize, however, are the racist elements embedded in the very fabric of our culture—the mass of "knowledge" that is passed on, often informally, from generation to generation.

Each of us carries around more accumulated residue from the past than we are ordinarily aware of. Whenever I am able to observe my own thoughts with what seems like complete honesty, I am appalled at the stereotypes that come forth as I deal with people of a race, gender, religion, or political view different from my own. A deeply held opposition to prejudice and discrimination usually causes me to reject or supersede such thoughts as they arise, but I have no doubt that my behaviors are often shaped, even slightly, by them when I am not being conscious.

Shifting prejudices for the moment, I will admit that whenever I meet a woman in a powerful position in business or government, my mind brings forth a set of stereotypes about such women lacking femininity, hating men, being grasping and greedy, and so forth. Realize that I do not believe these stereotypes are truthful, and I would never knowingly act on such stereotypes. In fact, I am willing to disparage people who do believe and act on such stereotypes. (I hereby disparage all such people.)

Still, having proclaimed what a wonderfully liberal and nonchauvinist person I am, the fact remains that all of those stereotypes and more are stored somewhere in my mind and that they automatically are brought to the surface whenever the circumstances suggest their relevance. I have no memory of personal experiences that would have led me to form such conclusions about powerful women. I don't even remember anyone teaching me these views. Because I am quite sure no one is playing subliminal hate tapes through my pillow at night, I have concluded that I simply have soaked them up from the pool of such views pervading our society. I suspect, moreover, that I am not alone.

The power of institutional bigotry is difficult to grasp because so much of it is invisible, unconscious, and, even in the case of the ugliest stereotypes, officially disavowed. We can recognize the overt prejudice and discrimination of individuals; we can disparage it and argue against it; but it is far more difficult to recognize and deal with institutional bigotry.

In recent years, the notion of "a level playing field" has been advanced as the proper way to deal with racial inequities. It is offered as an explicit alternative to affirmative action programs, which are based on the view that previously disadvantaged groups deserve some degree of compensatory assistance today to make up for past discrimination. The new notion typically includes an admission of regret over past evils, a promise not to do it anymore, and a request simply to "let bygones be bygones."

This is a compelling suggestion, reflected in the tearful plea of victim Rodney King in the wake of the Los Angeles riots: "Can't we just get along?" Unfortunately we cannot simply proclaim a level playing field anymore than a sexually active person can decide to be a virgin from now on. As we'll see, it is possible to change culture, but it cannot be accomplished by simple proclamation.

During the 1990s, we are witnessing the attempt to transform the economies of nations formerly comprising the Soviet bloc. The shift from socialism to capitalism is a difficult one, however; obstacles are more fundamental than were necessarily appreciated. Flores (1991) observes:

> Russian children do not (yet) see the possibility of setting up lemonade stands as American children do. We suggest that this difference arises because American children live in a culture permeated by practices for selling and buying things. Our children are surrounded by friends, siblings and neighbors that have built lemonade stands that they can imitate. They are acting out of a complex web of interconnected skills learned by trading toys, shopping with their parents, and so on. The possibility of buying, selling and owning things is just part of the way they see the world. (p. 6)

When Poland returned to competitive pricing after many years, it was reported that people were at a loss to take advantage of the free market. They knew that certain stores were charging less, but they had no skills for shopping around. Their experience of stores was not about comparison shopping; it was about standing in line. A person who has never experienced a market economy could read a roomful of books about capitalism and still not know how to shop.

SOCIAL STRUCTURE IS EVERYWHERE

The purpose of this chapter has been to draw your attention to the reality of *social structure:* those nontangible patterns of social life that importantly affect you and everyone you know. Social structure shapes your behavior; it conditions your beliefs, values, and opinions. Social structure is a grid that defines who you are—both in the ways you are identified by others and in how you *feel* about yourself.

Social structure is a powerful *presence* that fills the space around you, no matter where you are. If you are indoors right now, it fills the room you are in. If you happen to be outdoors, that presence surrounds you, extending out from you in all directions. You cannot escape it because you bring it with you wherever you go. This presence is like a grand, invisible puppeteer, quietly tugging the strings attached to your arms and legs, strings that affect your body language and facial expressions, strings that cause the words you speak, and strings that reach even into your mind and control your thoughts, including the thoughts you are having right now about what I just said.

Take a moment to pause right now. Put down the book and observe the thoughts you are having. See whether you can trace any of those thoughts to things you have been taught or to things you have just come to believe as you grew up. If anything I've said makes you feel uneasy or angry, if it simply doesn't make sense in terms of what you know about reality, then you are confronting aspects of social structure right now. Take a moment now to look at your thoughts.

Notice how difficult it is to observe your thoughts and to analyze them, because observation and analysis are acts of thinking. Perhaps you can notice some ways in which the established beliefs you have come to accept now govern how you think about your thoughts and about social structure. For example, if you found yourself worrying about how the discussion of social structure relates to any religious beliefs you may have—especially if you found yourself rejecting anything I said in the fear that it might contradict those religious beliefs—you were face to face with the presence we are trying to observe and understand. For your present peace of mind, please know that I will never ask you to give up any of those beliefs.

If you found yourself thinking that some of the notions I've put forth conflict with things you've been told by people you respect—parents, teachers, peers—those very thoughts and any concerns that accompanied the thoughts are part of the creature we are tracking down. Realize that this investigation does not require you to abandon anyone you have come to respect.

Or perhaps you found yourself worrying about psychological problems such as schizophrenia or just panicked that thoughts like the ones you were thinking would make you crazy. Any difficulty you have in looking into social structure the way I am suggesting to you probably illustrates the *recursive* quality that I mentioned earlier. It's a little like turning around to see the back of your head. Ultimately we are trying to think about something that controls our thinking. Far from making you crazy, however, success in this venture can make you sane.

I do not suggest that social structure as this invisible presence controls your thoughts and actions totally, but there is a greater danger that you will *under*estimate its impact, rather than *over*estimate it. To the extent that you are unconscious of its presence and power, you are at risk of being its slave. My purpose in this book, then, is to help you reveal the presence of social structure to yourself because this is one of those situations in which the truth can literally set you free.

CONCLUSION

Social structure is real. Even though it is intangible, it exercises a powerful influence in your life. In this chapter, we examined some of the elements (e.g., statuses, roles, norms, values, institutions) of social structure, as well as some of the forms it can take (e.g., relationships, groups, organizations, societies).

We have begun to take seriously the notion that social structure exists separate from any specific human beings, including those who created it in the first place. In Chapter 3, we will look at the substance of social structure—what it's made of—and its purposes.

Points of Discussion

- What thoughts, if any, come into your mind and interfere with the inquiry I've been suggesting? Which thoughts can you connect to aspects of social structure? Explain.

- I've said that norms and sanctions are designed to apply and enforce our shared values. Sometimes, however, the values change, but the norms and sanctions are so firmly established that they continue in force. Describe some examples of this.

- Describe the different cultures that distinguish some of the organizations you are familiar with: different fraternities and sororities, different social service clubs, different athletic teams, for example.

Reading Further

Jack Levin's *Sociological Snapshots* (Newbury Park, CA: Pine Forge, 1993) draws your attention to the presence of social structure in all corners of everyday life. Topics include American concerns about being fat, soap operas, the baby boom generation, aging, rumors, and mass murder. This is a very readable book, intended for a general audience.

John Naisbitt and Patricia Aburdene's *Re-Inventing the Corporation* (New York: Warner, 1985) will offer you an opportunity to compare some old and new views of how modern organizations operate.

As we continue our examination of social structure, we'll frequently focus our attention on organizations as concrete examples. The business of running an organization brings you face to face with its existence as a system separate from the individual humans involved. You might appreciate Jane Hannaway's many insights into this phenomenon in her *Managers Managing: The Workings of an Administrative System* (New York: Oxford University Press, 1989).

CHAPTER THREE

Freedom and Society

Social structure is a social creation, not some kind of genetic inheritance. In this chapter, we see some of the reasons for creating social structure and what it's made of.

We've talked about social structure for two chapters. Now I want to take up a rather fundamental question: What is social structure made of?

It will be useful to deal at the outset with some things that social structure may seem like but is not. For example, whenever I've asked students what social structure is made of, the most common and immediate answer is "people." Although human beings are involved in social structure, people are not the *substance* of it.

When I've asked this same question of my sociology colleagues, they tend to answer most often "social statuses and roles," which are discussed in Chapter 2. Although this answer is nearer the truth, I would suggest that the substance of social structure is organized and structured in the form of statuses and roles but that the substance itself is something else.

To find out what social structure is really made of, I will take you on a slightly circuitous route.

A SOCIOBIOLOGICAL DETOUR

A number of years ago, a group of scholars at Harvard and elsewhere committed a terrible academic sin: They trespassed on collegial turf. Essentially a group of biologists suggested that all of the phenomena that social scientists had been grappling with for centuries could be explained fairly simply as a matter of biology. The idea didn't fly very well among social scientists.

For the most part, E. O. Wilson (1978) and his colleagues suggested that many of the lessons learned in animal studies could apply quite nicely to human behavior as well. In a discussion of altruism, for example, Wilson suggested that the kinds of self-sacrificing behavior we often celebrate as honorable could be traced to and accounted for by a genetically wired instinct to perpetuate our human gene pool.

Thus, when a mother rushes into a burning building to save her baby, we tend to explain that as a matter of motherly love, and we understand when similar behavior occurs among other sets of relatives or other intimate relationships. Most people would say it's a matter of love and let it go at that; sociologists and psychologists, however, might venture to suggest how people come to understand what love involves, talking perhaps of role models who instill images in our minds of how we ought to behave.

I don't think any sociologist (I can't speak for psychologists and other social scientists) would ever suggest that the mother rushing into the burning building to save her baby (a) didn't have a choice and (b) didn't deserve our admiration for her heroism. Yet that's pretty much what the sociobiologists were saying. To the extent that sociobiology was known about outside academia, it didn't have great press among the general public either.

Unquestionably, I think, much of the opposition to sociobiology—both lay and academic—rested on its implicit and explicit denial of free will. It paints a picture of human behavior that is as mindlessly deterministic as a stream of army ants giving their bodies to death by drowning in a stream so that those farther back in the column will be able to walk across the accumulation of corpses.

The objections to sociobiology were not only emotional, however. A number of thoughtful critics raised important theoretical and methodological issues. For example, the empirical basis for the theory rests on studies on nonhumans only. Although such studies can provide insights into humans, they are never definitive. Also sociobiology tends to ignore the wide range of differences across societies—in mother-child relationships, for example.

Whatever its fundamental flaws, sociobiology has some real value for the present discussion. It opens the possibility that human behavior occurs in response to a causal dynamic operating at some level other than that of individual human needs and desires. The fundamental flaw made by the sociobiologists, I think, was their assumption that they had discovered the only game in town; the flaw in categorical opposition to sociobiology was to deny the game existed at all.

I suggest that there is indeed more here than meets the eye, but it is of a very different nature from what was perceived by the sociobiologists.

THE POSSIBILITY OF FREEDOM

In the matter of free will and determinism, for example, suppose that human beings fundamentally possess free choice but often act as though they don't. Suppose some dynamic is operating that tends to make humans behave in the ways that the sociobiologists would interpret as a sign of no free will. Here is an example.

Imagine a group of children playing a game of baseball on a balmy summer afternoon. A young man of 10, with images of glory in his mind, steps to the plate. He taps it a couple of times with the tip of his bat and looks up, into the steely eyes of a young woman of 11, glaring down at him from the pitcher's mound. She has images of glory decorating her mind too, and there's no room there for a happy batter.

The first pitch is swung on and missed; the second is fouled back over the head of the catcher. The young batter steps back from the plate and studies his bat for defects. The pitcher twists the ball around in her hand, never taking her eyes away from the batter, who feigns surprise at finding no holes in his bat.

Now comes the windup and the pitch: strike three. The batter mutters something we can't hear clearly, looks down at his feet, and leaves the batter's box, shuffling off to the sidelines.

Here's the point of this story of victory and defeat. The young man relinquishes his turn at bat despite the fact that we'd all agree it is more fun to bat (granted, he may be having some second thoughts about that) than to stand idly by watching the action.

Now notice that the young batter *could* have stayed in the batter's box. Free will would have allowed that. Only the rules of the game disallow it. However, the batter in this instance (and in all similar instances) behaves as though his free will did not reach far enough to allow his staying at bat beyond three strikes. We would all agree his free will would not permit him to flap his arms and become airborne. At this moment of personal crisis, he is acting exactly as though his free will was equally impotent in the matter of batting after three strikes.

An observer from Mars (which some suggest may explain the sociobiologists) might very well conclude that although human beings possess a degree of free will, it does not extend to the point of batting (or attempting to bat) after racking up three strikes. Actually the observer from Mars might conclude (as the sociobiologists did) that human beings don't have very much free will, if any, though the careful observer would note peculiar variations in the automaticity of human behavior.

Hovering over Wellington, Sydney, Kuala Lumpur (or most portions of the planet, for that matter), our Martian sociologist would conclude that human beings were incapable of driving automobiles on the right-hand side of the road, whereas an observer swooping down over San Diego and Tijuana would report back an astonishing finding: *Some humans are incapable of driving on the left-hand side of the road.*

FREEDOM AS POSSIBILITY

Freedom is really a matter of possibilities or options. When I say, "You are free to leave," I mean that's an option you have. (Unless you were chained in place, of course, it's an option you had even without my permission.) When you think you have a choice between going to the movies or to the opera, you experience that possibility of choosing as a form of freedom.

And freedom is very important to us. When a robber sticks a gun in your back and says, "Give me your wallet," it's not that piece of cowhide and the picture of the cocker spaniel puppy that came with it that's really at stake. Ultimately it's not even the money but the freedom, in the form of possibilities or options, that the money affords you. It's the places you can go and the things you can do and eat that give the money its value.

Although we seem to value freedom highly and get upset at the suggestion that we are not free, we are downright schizophrenic about it. Take a moment to reflect on it, and you'll see that your life is filled with the possibility of freedoms that you consistently do not exercise. You could eat mashed potatoes with your hands, but don't. You could stroll down Main Street naked, but don't. You could wear blue jeans to your boss's formal dinner, but you dress up instead. You could drink a cocktail made of equal parts of 1947 Chateau Lafitte Rothschild, root beer, and lemonade, but . . . (Warning: Do not try this at home.)

The truth is, we give away our freedom every day in damn near every way. Let's look at some examples. Consider some of the ways we give away our freedom through our language.

"You make me so angry." (In other words, I don't have any control over my anger; you control me in that respect.)

"You made me love you." (Musical tribute to lack of freedom.)

"I couldn't help myself." (Enough said.)

"I couldn't tell my own mother that."

"I could never work for a company that did that."

"I didn't have a choice."

The disavowal of freedom embedded in the idioms of our language is merely the tip of the iceberg. We behave accordingly, as well. Habits are a good example. Rather than choose our behavior each moment, we fall into patterns of unconscious repetitions. Habits are a way of putting ourselves on automatic pilot.

Habits let us exist without the need for freedom. Our personal, human habits have numerous analogues in life. Computer programs are a great example. If you were an accountant, you could sit down at a calculator and laboriously create a table detailing 30 years of monthly mortgage payments ($200,000 at 8.8% interest), indicating the portion of each payment counting against the principal and the portion going toward interest. Such a table would run several pages and would take hours to create.

Now imagine that you complete the task, only to discover you should have used 8.9%. It would take hours more to create the new table. We can fairly easily teach a computer the habits involved in the routine calculations that result in the table of mortgage payments. Having created the program, it is a trivial matter to create the payment table at 8.8%, 8.9%, 8.7%, and so on. Just as easily, you could compare the implications of a $200,000 loan, a $220,000 loan, one for $180,000, and so on. It's so trivial for a computer to perform what were once laborious tasks, that you can indulge yourself the fantasy of borrowing $200,000,000 or $2,000,000,000—experimenting with a variety of interest rates.

If computer programs provide a clear analogy to our tendency toward habits, so did the whole Industrial Revolution much earlier. Whereas the creation of products such as woven goods, furniture, or automobiles required humans to perform specific actions repeatedly, it became possible to create machines to perform those same tasks. Machines are good at habits; in fact, that's their best way of being. (When a machine kicks a habit, we say it's "broken.")

The invention of the servo-mechanism (building feedback into the loop of habit) brought machines up to the level of freedom at which most humans operate most of the time. Now a machine can (a) shave a layer of wood off a board, (b) measure its thickness, (c) find it too thick, (a) shave off another layer, (b) measure its thickness, and so on.

When sophisticated machines first were invented and began to put humans out of work, one justification for the industrial/computer revolution was that machines would take over the repetitive drudgery of life, while humans would be liberated for more creative pursuits: writing poetry, inventing more humane social structures, and so on.

How well has it worked? Not as we planned, I would suggest. Rather than devote ourselves to creative pursuits, we are more inclined to form new habits. One of our inventions—the clock—has powerfully aided our rush to regularity. It lets us rise at the same time each day, perform the same morning functions in the same order, go to the same job at the same time by the same means to do the same work the same way . . .

Nor is the habituality habit limited to work. We establish straitjackets for our "spare time" as well. For many Americans, another invention— television—has helped regularize our evenings. How many people have an iron-clad commitment about what they watch at 9:00 on Monday nights? Some people watch professional football as faithfully every Sunday as others go to church at the same time. Both are operating out of habit rather than by choice.

Sometimes we take a certain pride in our habitual character. Often we use our habits as bases of our identities. We like being known as the person who gets up early . . . or late. Some are known as "not worth a damn before that first cup of coffee in the morning," while others settle into a health niche of being opposed to coffee and other desecrations of the bodily temple. It isn't so important *what* we are but *that* we are. Somehow our habits vouch for our existence. Eccentric habits, at least, can cause other people to talk about us, and when they do that, it gives us extra proof of our existence.

Although we say we treasure freedom, then, we also give it away at the drop of a hat. As we'll see now, that waiver makes society possible.

GUARANTEES OF FREEDOM

Why is it that Americans, with our much vaunted and cherished freedom of religion, with the constitutionally guaranteed right to choose what- ever religion we want, so overwhelmingly choose the same religion as our parents? We could understand this behavior among natives of some preliterate tribe, who don't know about other religious possibilities. But why is this the case in America?

When you look at the history of our constitutional guarantees, you will discover that our freedom of religion was not designed as a freedom of choice. It was not envisioned as a freedom to change. In fact, it was primarily a freedom *not* to change—a freedom to stay the same. The First Amendment in the Bill of Rights actually guarantees that no one will be forced by the state to adopt a different religion from one of his or her parents. That we have the freedom to change from what we have been socialized into is an unintended by-product of the First Amendment and one we seldom take advantage of.

Although we tend to see our constitutional guarantee regarding religion as a liberal orientation, it is actually more conservative. It is a promise that we will not have to change, regardless of what the king or the president might like.

Although we tend to think that the Constitution puts power in the hands of the individual, it actually focuses power in the hands of socialization units smaller than the nation-state, most notably in families of birth and peer groups. Those smaller socialization units are as demanding of conformity as any other, however, and they are actually more effective at getting it. Freedom is surrendered less often to the guns of armies and police than to the stern look of a mother.

The Constitution never mentions the individual, interestingly enough. It does not actually guarantee any freedoms to the individual; it merely restricts the federal government's ability to take freedoms away. By the same token, the perennial question of "states' rights" in America is really a question of whether the public officials running state governments can take away any individual freedoms not taken away by the federal government.

It has been my experience that when students first confront the extent to which they are giving away their freedom, a kind of panic sets in. Often they will resist what I have been saying by demanding to know whether I expect them to break with all of the social conventions they have been surrendering to: Should they run naked in the park?

Once I've noted that they are merely trying to give *me* their freedom instead of giving it to the customary recipients, I do suggest that they remain clothed. In fact, I suggest that *you* begin by keeping all of the agreements you've previously made; that is, for the time being, keep giving your freedom away just as you have been doing previously—except that now you know you are doing it. Know that you are surrendering your freedom, not that you are doing things because you have to. *Choose* to do them. This is one of the few situations in which the truth can truly set you free. You cannot regain and retain your freedom as long as you believe it is being taken away from you; your power comes from the recognition that you are the one giving it away. It just makes sense: If you are giving it away, you can stop. If someone is taking it away successfully against your will, you would appear to be helpless in the matter.

Let's also be clear that I am not talking about some form of nihilistic, total freedom. The freedom you possess as a human being is a lot like money. Its only value lies in your ability to use it. Whereas money gets its value through our spending it, we "spend" our freedom in the creation of social structure. So, just as there may be something therapeutic about lighting a cigar with a $100 bill, maybe it would do you good to run naked through the park now and then. But neither works as a way of life. Mostly you spend your money on "sensible" things like food and underwear, and mostly you spend your freedom to create society.

THE SUBSTANCE
OF SOCIAL STRUCTURE

This lengthy discussion of individual freedom and our tendency to give it away has a specific purpose. We are now ready to see what social structure is made of.

Social structure is made of the freedom of individuals. *Surrendered freedom is the substance of society.* If you were to create some new social structure, you would need to get individual human beings to give up portions of their freedom—some of the options and possibilities they would otherwise enjoy. The truth is, of course, that you have created social structure throughout your life, and you have done that by getting other human beings to surrender portions of their freedom. Let's look at a simple example.

Imagine that you and I have just met, at work perhaps, and we each decide we would like to get to know the other a little better. I suggest we have lunch. When you and I agree to meet at Chez Ptomaine for lunch at noon on Tuesday, we each have agreed to give up a bit of our freedom—that is, the freedom to do something else at that time. In the process, we have created a new social entity—or the potential for one—a luncheon party. When I call for reservations, we become "the Babbie party." When we are seated at lunch, we will be "the party at Table 13." Notice how we will have become something more than two individuals; we are a social entity. That entity was created from our individual freedom.

SAVING THE SKEETS

Here's a slightly more complicated example of how we create social entities by surrendering our freedom. Suppose we individually happen to enjoy listening to "Car Talk" on National Public Radio (a humorous program of automobile advice) and have become concerned about the program's crusade to "Save the Skeet." Each of us individually forms an intention to raise money for the Clay Pigeon Trauma Center. So far, each of us can give up that intention in an instant and can even stop listening to Click and Clack, the Tappet brothers, altogether. In fact, nobody's holding a gun to your head to make you listen to the radio at all. Although you have a felt need to raise money for the suffering skeets, you have a lot of freedom in that regard.

In the course of getting to know one another at lunch, we discover our mutual passion. Quickly we decide we could be much more powerful in concert than individually. We make a pact to form the Peoria Chapter of the Save the Skeet Foundation and begin planning activities aimed at raising money for the Clay Pigeon Trauma Center.

To strengthen our resolve and to become more potent, we elect officers—you are elected president after 37 consecutive tie votes. (I was in the bathroom during the 38th balloting.) We plan our first organizational meeting: for Thursday night at 7:30, at my home. We each agree to invite 10 people to the meeting. Furthermore, we agree that I will let you invite people from work, and I will focus on my bowling league.

Notice the tangled web we've begun to weave, without even trying to deceive. Thursday night is pretty much gone, as far as freedom is concerned. Moreover, we've each committed some portion of our time to inviting people to the meeting, and I've further committed myself to talking to the bowling league, whom I'm now beginning to suspect may not be all that sympathetic to the plight of clay pigeons anyway. Chances are, in fact, that I will get a lot of ribbing from the other bowlers—many of whom belong to the National Rifle Association—and I might (worst case) be drummed out of the league.

Had I been operating on my own up to now, I could chuck the whole thing, on more sober reflection. But now, of course, I've made a commitment to you. It's more difficult backing out at this point. That's the difference between simply having an idle thought and surrendering freedom through a set of agreements. I don't mean to cry about what you've done to me, by the way. I know you now have your own problems. Whereas I'm faced with expulsion from the bowling league (and I was never that good anyway), you've committed yourself to being at risk at work. You may come out of this misadventure with a damaged job situation.

Now look at this situation from a slightly different perspective. Let's consider the clay pigeons' interests for a moment. By surrendering portions of our freedom and making commitments to one another, we have created something more potent on behalf of the defenseless skeets than existed when you and I each had our individually bleeding heart.

Making a bit of a conceptual jump, I suggest that the work of society, as well as its very survival, depends on our surrendering our freedom, even though we are not always aware that's what we are doing.

Let's stay with the Peoria Chapter of the Save the Skeet Foundation for a moment. On Thursday night, 14 people come to our organizational meeting, we show a videotape about the death and destruction of clay pigeons, and 10 of the guests agree to join our club. That makes an even dozen of us.

One of the new members, an attorney, suggests that the club should have a set of bylaws specifying the club's mission, providing for the election and term of officers, setting the dues, determining who can authorize the expenditure of club monies, and so forth. She argues that bylaws will be particularly important if we go on to seek tax-exempt status from the state so we can each deduct our contributions at tax time. Moreover, she volunteers to draft the bylaws.

With only the slightest of collective trepidation (and two abstentions), we vote to let her do it. We have now at least committed ourselves to considering the bylaws and possibly the issue of tax-exempt status. If we later pass the bylaws, we will have further constrained our freedom. Each of us individually will have been increasingly "roped in," and our loss is probably the clay pigeons' gain because we are now more likely to do something of impact.

It is useful to consider some of the many subtle ways we've lost our freedom. I guess it goes without saying that each of the 12 of us has given up the possibility of going trapshooting on the weekend. Moreover, we are kind of committed to giving up friends who may take a hostile attitude toward clay pigeons. At the very least, we can't bring them around our other friends.

Thursday nights are pretty much gone now. Except for the possibility of videotaping it, we have given up the freedom to watch "A Treasury of Shi'ite Humor" from 8:00 to 8:05. In the process, we will have lessened the possibility of ever engaging in humorous repartee with Muslim fundamentalists. Soon, moreover, we are committing ourselves to club events outside of regularly scheduled meetings, such as picketing the local country club on weekends.

Step by step, we have invested more and more freedom into the corporate enterprise we've created. And notice that freedom really is the fundamental substance of organizations such as this. When we say we ~~ our time, we are really saying that we've given up the freedom to ~~ in other ways. The same holds for money: The dues we pay ~~ oss of freedom to spend the money on something else.

Although our surrendered freedom is the fundamental substance of organizations, that's not all we've invested in the local chapter of the Save the Skeet Foundation. We've also invested a portion of our identity and even, in a sense, some measure of our perceived self-worth. For our friends at work, the foundation is that thing you and I belong to. If it one day wins the Nobel Peace Prize (Amnesty International and the Red Cross have won it), then you and I gain some personal prestige in the purpose. If the national scandal sheets reveal that saving the skeets was all a joke from the start, then we look stupid and silly. Our investment of self-identity can be seen from two directions. On the one hand, the organization becomes associated with us; on the other, we think of and identify ourselves with it. That affiliation—that investment of freedom—becomes a part of our self-image, who we think we are. In a sense, we are saying, "I am someone who cares about clay pigeons." That is likely to spill over into other aspects of our self-image: that we are "caring people" more generally, and that, in turn, may result in other forms of behavior. We may find ourselves joining other organizations to protect other inanimate objects.

THE PURPOSES OF SOCIAL STRUCTURE

The preceding discussion illustrates some of the ways we invest our individual freedom in social structure. The Save the Skeets example also illustrates a common, but not universal, aspect of the investment: Often we create social structure for a purpose. Sometimes we organize for altruistic purposes; at other times we do it to make money.

The purposefulness of social structure can be seen also in terms of the elements discussed in Chapter 2. The norm of driving on the right-hand side of the road has the purpose of enhancing traffic safety. The custom of giving gifts at weddings has the purpose of helping establish a household for the newly married couple. We establish tax laws for the purpose of raising money to cover the costs of government. We create governments "to form a more perfect union, establish justice, insure domestic tranquility, provide for the common defense, promote the general welfare and secure the blessings of liberty" (to borrow from a well-known body of social structure). Nations sign treaties to ensure their mutual defense.

Without denying the informal and hidden purposes operating in various elements and forms of social structure, the earliest sociological studies of formal organizations took a rational, goal-attainment view pretty much for granted. This is evident, for example, in Max Weber's classic study of bureaucracy (see Weber, 1925/1946, pp. 196-244).

The Rationalist View of Social Structure

Although we tend to complain a great deal about bureaucracy today, especially its stupidities and inefficiencies, it is worth noting that the development of bureaucracy was seen initially as a progressive step in each of those regards. Prebureaucratic organizations, such as governments and businesses, were run at the whim of autocratic leaders, as Weber (1925/1946) reminds us. The king or feudal lord had total control over operations within his domains. Moreover, these rulers acquired such autocratic positions because of inheritance or military prowess, not on the basis of their abilities to administer organizations. By contrast, bureaucracy was to these earlier forms of organization as mass production was to cottage industry. Here are some of the elements of bureaucracy that attracted Weber's attention. Notice how each fits into the model of a machine with interchangeable parts.

- *Specified Functions:* Each individual in a bureaucracy has formally specified duties and responsibilities. If you were to join a bureaucratic office, you would assume specific functions already established.

- *Authority Structure:* Who reports to whom, who can give orders, and who has to take them—all such issues are established formally. When a new person joins a bureaucratic office, there is no need for "jockeying for power" because power relations already are specified.

- *Established Procedures:* The ways specific situations are to be dealt with are established formally. If you want to insure an airmail package at the post office, it shouldn't matter which clerk is on duty, because the procedures are the same in any case. By the same token, a Big Mac™ in Toledo is the same as a Big Mac™ in Santa Fe.

- *Recorded Files:* The operations of the organization are recorded in files that are stored and can be referred to easily. If you need to discuss your tax return with the Internal Revenue Service, any agent should be able to locate your records and deal with your needs. Nothing depends on the memory of specific staff members.

Although we have been considering bureaucracy primarily at the ⌐ ⌐ single office, huge complex organizations can be seen in a ⌐n. As Gareth Morgan (1986, p. 27) describes the situation, ⌐tion is conceived as a network of parts: functional departments such as production, marketing, finance, personnel, and research and development, which are further specified as networks of precisely defined jobs."

Seen thusly, especially in contrast to administrative alternatives, bureaucracy certainly seems like an intelligent way to organize human operations. Like the technological innovations in industry, bureaucracy seems modern, intelligent, and rational. Not surprisingly, many people have sought to expand and exploit its apparent potential.

Frederick the Great, king of Prussia from 1740-1786, envisioned an army in which each soldier was like a standardized part in a well-oiled machine. Morgan (1986, pp. 23-24) describes some of the steps Frederick took to accomplish that aim.

> In particular, Frederick was fascinated by the workings of automated toys such as mechanical men, and in his quest to shape the army into a reliable and efficient instrument, he introduced many reforms that actually served to reduce his soldiers to automata. Among these reforms were the introduction of ranks and uniforms, the extension and standardization of regulations, increased specialization of tasks, the use of standardized equipment, the creation of a command language, and systematic training which involved army drill. Frederick's aim was to shape the army into an efficient mechanism operating through means of standardized parts.

About a century later, Frederick Taylor, an American engineer, took the notion of human workers as parts in a machine several steps further. Early in the 20th century, he introduced the notion of *scientific management* (Taylor, 1911), aimed at achieving the maximum productivity from workers. In most respects, his methods involved turning the workers into cogs in a larger machine. Tasks were to be broken down into ever smaller parts, with each worker performing an ever simpler action repetitively. This repetition meant that workers didn't need to think about what they were doing or—worse yet—to make decisions. In fact, Taylor was explicit about shifting all decision making to the supervisors.

Scientific management, or *Taylorism*, as it came to be called, resulted in numerous innovations. "Time-and-motion studies," conducted by "efficiency experts," have been in vogue from time to time during this century. Typically such activities have produced resistance and resentment among those studied and made more efficient, and the whole enterprise has been widely ridiculed.

On the positive side, it should be noted that the field of *ergonomics*—the design of tools (such as chairs or computers) to better fit the hum body and mind—is also a logical extension of Taylorism. In more recent times, management by objectives (MBO) and planning, programming, budgeting systems (PPBS) are other manifestations of the notion that corporate human behavior can be put on a fully rational basis. Once an organization's aims have been clarified, according to this view, it is a relatively straightforward matter to develop the network of steps necessary for accomplishment. Often, however, the theory seems more effective than the practice.

Notice that when we view social structure as being rationally purposeful, our surrender of freedom makes good sense. We invest our freedom in ways that should satisfy our personal needs and desires. However, sociologists long ago realized that the purposes of social structure were not necessarily what they might seem. When the farm wives of an earlier era got together for quilting bees, more was involved than the production of bed covers. After all, they could have made quilts at home alone. The gossiping, however, was not incidental; it was a central purpose.

For many people, their work situation is much more for them than merely a way to earn a living. It can be an important focus of friendships that carry over to nonworking hours. Work can provide feelings of accomplishment, fulfillment, and importance. For some, work is an excuse to escape family members and responsibilities in the home.

The unofficial purposes that crop up in formal organizations can often interfere with the official purposes. Sometimes behavior within a corporation is guided more by friendship than by official duties and responsibilities: when friendship is the primary basis for promotions or other benefits, for example.

Similarly students go to college for the official purpose of becoming more educated, but the additional purposes are many: escape from parental authority, finding a spouse, athletics, carousing. For many, the importance of the educational purpose becomes eclipsed by the others.

On balance, then, contemporary sociologists are less inclined to see organizations as rational systems for accomplishing specified tasks than was previously the case. In part, this shift in focus has come from a growing recognition of the hidden agenda and nonrational aspects to individuals' behavior within formal organizations.

the same token, many examples of organizational behavior are tradition rather than efficiency. In the most modern, techno-to-date bureaucracy, you can still hear the comment, "But s done it that way!" as justification for behavior that makes urely rational eye. What other justification is there for the electoral college in modern American elections? Every 4 years, we flirt with the possibility that the candidate receiving the most popular votes will not take office, being supplanted by a candidate who actually received fewer popular votes.

The separation of social structure from human purposes can be extended far beyond issues of human forgetfulness or irrationality. We are about to make a shift of analysis that requires the kind of leap described in the earlier discussion of sociobiology. Instead of gene pools, however, we focus our attention on social structure as an entity unto itself.

Perhaps Our Purposes Are Irrelevant

It can be very useful to treat the elements and forms of social structure as entities in their own right. Rather than focus our attention on the aims and desires, we focus instead on the "purpose" pursued by the social structure itself. And, as we will see, the purpose of social structure as an entity is simply *survival.*

A modern paradigm for looking at organizations, for example, takes what is called a *population-ecology* point of view: It examines organizations as actors or entities in their own right. And whereas sociologists seek to understand human behavior in terms of the environmental forces that operate on individual humans, this new sociological paradigm takes a similar approach to understanding organizations.

Thus we can learn more about organizations if we take *their* point of view, rather than that of the human beings who create and comprise them. Just as we would seek to understand the voting behavior of an individual by recognizing the influence of his or her social class, religion, family background, and so on, so we can seek to understand what influences organizations to grow, shrink, innovate, retrench, and take other steps aimed at organizational survival. As Morgan (1986, p. 66) points out, "This 'population-ecology' view of organization brings Darwin's theory of evolution right into the center of organizational analysis."

Jitendra V. Singh (1990), in fact, speaks of organizational evolution in this context:

> The central theoretical thrust of organizational ecology is the investigation of how social environments shape rates of creation and death of organizational forms, rates of organizational founding and mortality, and rates of change in organizational forms. . . .

This book emphasizes organizational evolution, a broader theme.... Whereas ecology focuses on the relative demographic abundances of forms in relation to environmental conditions, evolutionary arguments are more interested in the dynamics of change in forms over time, especially how core structural properties of organisms influence their adaptation to changing environmental conditions. Ecological and evolutionary arguments ask complementary questions about the same historical processes. (pp. 11-12)

There is a potential danger in examining organizations and other forms of social structure by using concepts usually applied to humans. Whenever we treat organizations as entities, we tend to imbue them with human qualities. So we need to remember always the earlier assertion that "Human groups are not human." If we are to profit from examining social life from the point of view of organizations themselves, we cannot fall into the trap of thinking organizations will "see" things the way humans do.

We must guard against seeking the "psychology" of organizations because that is an anthropomorphic (human-centered) concept. We need to avoid slipping into thoughts about the "desires," "aims," or "fears" of organizations, for example. Nonetheless organizations and other forms of social structure operate in terms of discoverable patterns and "laws." They are just different from those that govern the behavior of humans.

The remainder of this book focuses on the behavior of organizations and other forms and elements of social structure as entities, with special attention to the drive for survival. In the course of that investigation, we see how social structure differs from human beings and how the two relate to one another.

CONCLUSION

Social structure is made of surrendered freedom. Equating freedom with options or possibilities, we saw that social structure is created from the willingness of individual human beings to give up some of the possibilities they enjoy. As we saw, however, humans are quite willing to give up freedom.

After examining some of the purposes humans have in mind when they create social structure, we considered the possibility that our purposes might not be as important as we thought. This chapter opened the issue of social structure having its own purpose: survival. In Chapter 4, we examine the survival mechanisms of social structure in some detail.

Points of Discussion

- Probably all of us have had the experience of being trapped by the commitments we have made to participate in organizations or other aspects of social structure. Recall some such experiences. What feelings did you have?

- What are some personal examples that illustrate the idea of social structure being made of surrendered individual freedom?

- What are the purposes of some of the organizations you participate in? Are they organized around the accomplishment of some rational objective or of something else? Do any of them have an "official" purpose but really seem to exist or operate for some other reason?

Reading Further

Sigmund Freud's classic *Civilization and Its Discontents* (New York: Norton, 1930/1961), edited and translated by James Strachey, offers an intriguing speculation about the origins of society. He lays out the dilemma of civilization as a two-edged sword: restricting our freedom, but also protecting it.

Jitendra V. Singh's *Organizational Evolution: New Directions* (Newbury Park, CA: Sage, 1990) brings together essays that illustrate the view of organizations as entities. Here you'll see how environmental factors influence the birth, change, and death of organizations, without reference to the hopes and aspirations of the individuals involved in them.

George Ritzer, in *The McDonaldization of Society* (Newbury Park, CA: Pine Forge, 1993), offers several fascinating views of modern culture. In particular, he is concerned with the extent to which the rationality that Weber (1925/1946) found exemplified in bureaucracy is equally well represented by the McDonald's fast-food chain. Moreover, Ritzer finds that Weber's fears about the dehumanization associated with the "iron cage" of rationality are also fully present in McDonald's and in all other aspects of modern American society that have been influenced by McDonald's.

CHAPTER FOUR

Structured for Survival

Here we learn about the special quality that turns organizations and other forms of social structure into entities in their own right—a transformation that gives them a beingness that extends beyond the control and perhaps the intentions of the humans who created them. Having created something that has our surrendered freedom as its substance, we see now that we've created freedom-taking machines.

In 1956, Leon Festinger and his colleagues (Festinger, Riecken, & Schacter, 1956) spent some time studying a flying saucer cult organized around a belief that a fleet of space vehicles was going to land on the earth for the purpose of evacuating a small group of humans prior to the destruction of the planet. The cult recruited volunteers from among family and friends for the survivor group. Festinger's team of psychologists also joined, for the purpose of studying the phenomenon.

The organizational crisis that most interested the researchers also gave the resulting book its title: *When Prophecy Fails*. Periodically the cult leaders would announce a date for the extraterrestrial pickup, and the members would close out all of their earthly affairs and repair to a local mountaintop that had been designated for embarkation. Then, after waiting all night in the cold, the members would trudge back to their earthbound lives to resume their day-to-day affairs. Festinger and his team were interested particularly in how people behave under such extreme conditions of *cognitive dissonance:* when their beliefs collide with reality.

The simplest of psychological models would have suggested the that group would fold after such an encounter. If you can imagine yourself in that situation, you'd probably say, "That's it, Jack. The world didn't come to an end, and I feel cheated. I'm out of here." What the researchers found, however, was just the opposite. Every such failure of prophecy—

and there were several—was followed by an intensified period of prose-lytization. They would try all the harder to get new members. Festinger's team tried to make sense of it all in terms of individual psychology—which they perhaps can be excused for by virtue of their being psychologists and not knowing any better.

There is certainly another perspective from which to view the events: There was a direct threat to the survival of the group, and it responded in defense; end of discussion. It's as simple as saying that I put my hand on the hot stove, it hurt, and I took my hand off. If we recognize that the cult members had formed a separate entity committed to its own survival, then we should look to see how it would behave in such a situation. It wouldn't seek survival out of emotions such as fear and loathing, but just because that's its nature. Organizations and other forms of social structure are constructed to seek survival by getting and keeping members and in other ways that we'll examine in this chapter.

AN AMAZING CONCEPT

In February 1982, I had the good fortune to attend a series of lectures given in San Francisco by the Chilean biologist Humberto Maturana. This probably seems an odd reference for a book on social structure, but Maturana said something in those lectures that has important implications for our present examination. Maturana introduced the term *autopoiesis* to explain the functioning of biological life. He defined it as "self-creation." A key feature of life, then, was that it was organized to create and re-create itself.

Autopoiesis is what distinguishes a social group from an audience or other aggregation. When people gather on the street to listen to an itinerant preacher or a politician, that gathering has no mechanism for its own survival. Even though the spectators at an NFL Super Bowl game can experience something very powerful as a corporate body—chanting, doing the wave, and so on—during the game, their groupness has no survival power. After the game is over and the fans have dispersed, the gathering no longer exists. This temporariness is why sociologists are careful to make the distinction between aggregations and groups.

Any instance of social structure has within it mechanisms for re-creating and perpetuating itself. It is, in that sense, self-sustaining. Here's an example of what I mean.

The British people are fond of saying, "There will always be an England," either to buoy themselves through adversity or sometimes in ironic reference to certain English eccentricities. Taken literally, however, the statement means there will always be a place occupied by people who identify themselves as English and who see themselves as the descendants of generations of others who considered themselves to be English. The problem, of course, is that all of the people who make England possible in this fashion keep dying, and the babies born in England don't even have the concept of England. However, British society is designed—through the operation of family, school, government, and other institutions—to socialize the young into their national identity, as well to teach them the need to replace themselves before they die and to socialize their replacements into their English identity. All societies are designed this way, which is why they persist as well as they do.

The autopoietic nature of society is more than simply a matter of survival, however. Autopoiesis is a matter of self-organization; as Maturana said, it's a matter of self-creation. This principle has important implications not only for the survival of society but also for the *study* of society.

Our task is to understand the organization of social life. This task is complicated, though, by the fact that the focus of study is not simply organized, but rather is always in the *process* of organizing itself. Moreover, we can carry out our study only from inside the midst of this self-organizing process. Finally, whatever we learn about the self-organizing process of society likely will affect the nature of that process. Hence whatever we learn may no longer be true as a consequence of our having learned it.

A SEMANTIC EXERCISE

Here's a simple analogy to illustrate the dilemma, suggested by Heinz von Foerster (1984, p. 7). Consider the following incomplete sentence:

THIS SENTENCE HAS _____ LETTERS.

Your task is to complete the sentence by filling in the blank (writing out a number in words) so that the completed sentence will be accurate. As you solve the puzzle, it is useful to notice the combination of deductive logic and inductive trial and error that may be appropriate to the task.

To begin deductively, we may reason that the completed sentence will have at least as many letters as are in it at the outset. The incomplete sentence has 22 letters. (Don't count the hyphen.) However, the sentence, THIS SENTENCE HAS TWENTY-TWO LETTERS actually has 31 letters, so that can't be the correct solution.

We could proceed in a purely inductive fashion from here, testing each possibility from 22 on up:

THIS SENTENCE HAS TWENTY-TWO LETTERS. (31)

THIS SENTENCE HAS TWENTY-THREE LETTERS. (33)

THIS SENTENCE HAS TWENTY-FOUR LETTERS. (32)

THIS SENTENCE HAS TWENTY-FIVE LETTERS. (32)

THIS SENTENCE HAS TWENTY-SIX LETTERS. (31)

THIS SENTENCE HAS TWENTY-SEVEN LETTERS. (33)

THIS SENTENCE HAS TWENTY-EIGHT LETTERS. (33)

THIS SENTENCE HAS TWENTY-NINE LETTERS. (32)

THIS SENTENCE HAS THIRTY LETTERS. (28)

Sometimes this kind of brute induction is the only way we can solve a problem, and computers have been invaluable in supporting that kind of inquiry. Sometimes, however, we can profit from just "winging it."

We are told that when Johannes Kepler was at work trying to fit Tycho Brahe's astronomical data to the Copernican notion that the earth and the other planets moved around the sun, he found that circular orbits didn't work, so he began looking for other geometric shapes. Butterfield (1960, p. 64) tells us that Kepler decided to try the ellipse as a temporary approximation of reality and found that it worked perfectly! Science often profits from serendipity in this fashion.

Suppose, in that spirit, we simply substitute THIRTY-ONE for TWENTY-TWO in the puzzle sentence. That turns out to be exactly right because the two numbers happen to have the same number of letters when they are written out. We have discovered the correct answer. Actually we have discovered *one* correct answer; there is another. If you continue inductively from this point, you soon will discover that THIS SENTENCE HAS THIRTY-THREE LETTERS is also correct.

If we were to continue pondering this word puzzle, you might be led to the realization that the sentence THIS SENTENCE HAS *SOME* LETTERS is also accurate. Now we would have increased the number of solutions from two to three. This innovation in the search, however, suggests some other possibilities, such as THIS SENTENCE HAS *MANY* LETTERS. How long will it be before we recognize the accuracy of such solutions as THIS SENTENCE HAS *MORE THAN TWO* LETTERS? The number of solutions has been inflated to infinity.

Notice the *recursiveness* of this process. Each of the statements we've considered has the recursive quality of creating its length in the course of asserting what that length is. Some such statements are accurate, others are not, but all such statements create their own lengths.

Other assertions have the autopoietic quality of creating the truth they assert just in the process of being asserted. Consider, for example, the assertion, "I apologize." Because an apology consists of saying, "I apologize," that statement becomes truth when you say it. Notice that the same cannot be said for the assertion, "I am sorry."

As we all know, you can say, "I'm sorry" when you really aren't sorry at all. In other words, you can lie by saying, "I'm sorry." Not so with, "I apologize." If you say it, you did it. The statement autopoietically creates what it says exists.

Notice that the statement "I am married" could be true or false. Some people say they're married when they're not, and others say they aren't when they are. But when the justice of the peace at Elvis's Blue Hawaii Chapel in Reno says, "I pronounce you husband and wife," it's a done deal. That's another autopoietic assertion. Other assertions become true by virtue of being uttered. Perhaps you can think of some.

Autopoiesis in human affairs does not end with semantics, however. In fact, it becomes more interesting when we shift our focus to other forms of behavior.

AUTOPOIETIC BEHAVIORS

Habits are autopoietic. I have the habit of getting up ridiculously early in the morning, weekends included. I say it's a habit because I do it almost all of the time. I wake up early even when I haven't set an alarm. Sometimes I promise myself that I'll sleep in, and I'm annoyed to find that I wake up early anyway. That definitely qualifies as a habit.

I say that habits are autopoietic because getting up early every morning not only *constitutes* a habit but also is what keeps me doing it. A habit is intrinsically designed for survival. The more you do it, the more habitual it becomes, and the more habitual it is, the more you do it. Take a moment to reflect on some of your habits. Maybe you always oversleep; maybe you always put your left shoe on before your right shoe; maybe you always say a prayer before exams. Whatever your particular pattern, notice that the more you do it, the more likely you are to do it in the future. Every time you do something because it's a habit, it becomes more of a habit.

Addictions are autopoietic. If you are addicted to cigarettes, that's explanation enough for why you are smoking. Anyone who has ever smoked regularly knows that. Yet, every time you smoke, the addiction becomes stronger. The same is true for alcohol. The more you drink, the more you want to drink, which makes it more likely that you will have another, which makes it more likely that you will want more . . .

The survival quality of habits and addictions is never more evident than when you try to break them. Try to quit smoking, and you'll find your body and mind screaming for a cigarette. It will be painfully obvious to you that you have created *something* with a "will to live" that is altogether independent of your desires, even though you are the one doing the smoking. The same autopoietic process occurs when we create social structure.

SOCIAL STRUCTURE SURVIVAL

Take a moment to think of some relationship you have with another person. Choose one that is fairly serious, not anything casual. It might be your relationship with a good friend, a romantic partner, or a parent.

Next think about some of the patterns that exist in your interactions with one another. For example, who is more likely to suggest things to do together during your leisure time? Who decides which movie to see? Who decides whether to eat out or stay in? Which one of you would be more likely to suggest taking a trip together?

Although you may have to make some adjustments to these questions to make them fit the relationship you are thinking of, my hunch is that you'll be able to recognize some differences in the roles that each of you plays in the relationship. All relationships are that way.

Now notice the similarity between the patterns of your relationship and the habits discussed earlier. If you are the one who always suggests going out to a movie, that pattern persists by virtue of your suggestions. Every time you say, "Let's go to a movie," the pattern becomes more habitual for the two of you, and that makes it more likely that you'll both abide by the pattern in the future. If you were suddenly to stop with your part of the pattern, you probably wouldn't see a movie for quite a while; your partner wouldn't think to suggest it.

If you reflect on it, you'll discover that you have formed numerous relationships involving autopoietic patterns. As the relationship becomes formed, each of you knows his or her roles in it. Anytime you try to break from those patterns, you may find resistance from your partner or at least an uneasy feeling of insecurity and uncertainty.

Other aspects of social structure exhibit this same autopoietic process for survival. Consider some common norms in our society. All college students know that when the instructor says, "If there are no further questions, you can leave a little early today," it is not appropriate to ask a question, especially a long and complicated one. That's one of those informal norms. I don't think it's written down anywhere (except here), and I'm quite sure it's not against the law to ask a question in that situation, yet it is a powerful norm that students rarely violate, and only at their peril.

The norm against asking last-minute questions survives from semester to semester by virtue of students honoring it. The reason they honor it is because it's such a firmly entrenched norm, which entrenches it all the more firmly.

It is also a norm to wear clothes in public. Although it is actually against the law to go naked in public, I suspect that you seldom think of the law when you dress each morning before you leave the house. The main power behind the norm is that everyone else is abiding by it. In other words, it is a norm primarily because everyone wears clothes, and you abide by the norm because everyone else is—making you one of those people creating the norm anew every day.

By now, you should be seeing the autopoietic quality in social structure. Notice that the bottom line in all of this is that social structure is designed to guarantee its own survival. It's not that social structure "wants" to survive; that's a human trait. It's simply designed that way.

So what does social structure need to survive? Let's consider organizations and nations as a way of illustrating some of the survival needs of social structural entities, in contrast to individual human beings.

Survival Needs

In this section, I want to illustrate some of the sociological attempts to determine what it takes for a social system to survive—without making a final assessment about the "correct" list. It is essential to distinguish social needs from individual needs. It should go without saying that social systems must satisfy certain needs of their individual human participants; in the extreme, if all humans died, the social structure would disappear as well.

In an even less extreme case, Morgan (1986, p. 43), for example, uses Abraham Maslow's (1943) hierarchy of human needs to focus on some of the ways a company must address the needs and desires of its employees. Whereas Maslow's hierarchy rests on a bedrock of physiological needs (food, shelter, etc.), Morgan points to wages and safe working conditions as ways an employer would help satisfy those human needs. Similarly Morgan sees health care programs and pension plans, guaranteed employment, and career paths within the organization as techniques of addressing the need for security, cited by Maslow (1943). Farther up the hierarchy, Morgan examines ways an organization could deal with the workers' social needs (e.g., office parties), ego needs (e.g., opportunities for achievement on the job), and self-actualization (jobs that serve as an expressive dimension in employees' lives).

Although satisfying the needs of human participants is vital to the survival of social structure, it is important to distinguish that aspect from the system needs of social structure. Indeed we need to look at the satisfaction of human needs strictly from the standpoint of the functions it serves for the system itself. At the same time, systems have survival needs that cannot be reduced to human needs.

In one of the best-known formulations of system imperatives, though also one of the most abstract, Talcott Parsons (1951) examined four basic needs: *Adaptation* involves the transformation and distribution of natural resources, with the economy being the primary instance of that function. *Goal attainment* refers to the system's need to establish priorities and to organize people to achieve them; government is the primary example of this need. *Integration* focuses on the coordination of the many parts making up the system, and Parsons (1951) says that laws are the chief vehicle for accomplishing that. Finally *latency* involves the maintenance of patterns of "proper" behavior. Parsons (1951) cites religion as an important institution for serving this function.

David Aberle and colleagues (Aberle et al., 1950, pp. 100-111), in contrast, provide a more concrete list of "functional prerequisites of a society":

an adequate relationship with the environment

provisions for sexual reproduction

the differentiation and assignment of roles

communication

shared views of things

shared values

norms regulating the means to achieving the goals

regulation of affective expression

socialization

effective control of disruptive behavior

Let's examine three system needs in a bit more depth to explore the intersection between individuals and social structure.

Replacement

No organization, no small neighborhood gang or large nation, can survive without members. Because all members eventually leave all organizations (at least by death), every organization needs *replacement* mechanisms. This need was discussed above with reference to the phrase "There will always be an England."

Happily humans have been designed, both physiologically and emotionally, to reproduce. Indeed the current state of overpopulation on the planet would suggest it is one of the things we do best—or at least most often.

In some cases, then, replacement is accomplished primarily by reproduction on the part of members. Children born into a particular nation or religion, for example, usually are brought up as members of it. Indeed one of the key distinctions between *sects* and *churches* in the sociological study of religion is that sects get new members through recruitment, while churches, being more established, can inherit theirs in the form of members' children.

If we examine human sexuality in practice around the world, however, we discover that it does not operate simply as what "comes naturally." Numerous rules pertain to how, when, and with whom: monogamy or polygamy, legally sanctioned marriages, common law marriages, or children born to and raised by single mothers. In some circumstances, members are encouraged to have large families for growth in the group overall; in others, members are encouraged to limit family size to stable replacement levels. In part, these rules reflect problems of competition, jealousy, and the like that arise from the unrestrained acting out of passion.

The bottom line here is that although replacement of group members can occur in many ways, this need must be met in some fashion or else the group will cease to exist. Reproduction is only a part of replacement, however.

Identity

Having members means something more than mere bodies. Any meaningful social group exists only when there are people who regard themselves as members of it, people who *identify* with it. Said somewhat differently, there must be people who identify themselves, in part, as members of the organization.

The problem is that newborn babies don't know whether they are Americans or Albanians, Baptists or Hindus, Raiders fans or Chargers fans. Nor do they have any idea what's expected of "people like them." Children must be educated, or *socialized,* into group membership. Sometimes this socialization occurs within nuclear families comprised of parents and their children or in extended families that include several generations. Sometimes group identity is learned in schools, peer groups, churches, or elsewhere. Typically it is a joint venture by several *agents of socialization.*

Although identification with organizations and other elements of social structure is sometimes a reasonably casual matter, often it is not. Usually, moreover, such identities are in opposition to other identities. Examples range from the Montagues and the Capulets of Shakespeare's *Romeo and Juliet* to the Crips and the Bloods of south central Los Angeles. Consider the Christians and the Muslims of the Crusades, or the Muslims and the Jews of today's Middle East. During the cold war, people who identified themselves with the nation of Yugoslavia did so partly in opposition to the capitalist nations of the West; with the thawing of cold war alliances and divisions, however, Yugoslavia devolved into bloodshed among people identifying themselves as Serbs, Croats, Bosnians, Slovenians, Macedonians, and Montenegrans, to name just a few.

Sometimes groups survive in the minds and hearts of people when those group identities have no formal existence. This was the case for the several ethnic groups that were bound together in the former Yugoslav republic, as well as the groups fighting each other in what were previously republics in the U.S.S.R. Similarly the Kurds regard themselves as a single people and comprised the nation of Kurdistan until the seventh century, but today these nomadic herders are "officially" citizens of Iraq, Turkey, Iran, Syria, or Armenia. Similar stories of group identity could be illustrated throughout Africa and other areas that experienced colonialization.

Decision-Making Structure

Organizations, nations, and other social groups need more than a mass of individuals who identify themselves as members of the group. Sociologists also agree on the need for some kind of group decision-making structure. Because an important part of group life involves acting in concert and/or agreeing to give up certain actions, some mechanism must exist whereby such agreements are established. In some cases, an individual, such as a powerful warrior or a hereditary ruler, dictates the "will of the group." You may not think very highly of such a system, but it should be noted that dictatorship serves the decision-making needs of organizations and that many nations have survived that way for long periods of time. Of course, aristocracy, theocracy, and democracy are but a few of the other political systems that also have been found to satisfy this need.

Smaller, less formal groups have the same need for group decision making. A small neighborhood gang or friendship clique must have some decision-making mechanism or else group action is impossible. Think about some such group that you may belong to or know about. There's a good chance that one person could be identified as the informal leader of the group—the person most likely to suggest group actions or perhaps the one who usually seems to have the first word in choosing among alternatives that have been suggested. Or if the group operates as a pure democracy, voting on every action, that's the provision the group has made for decision making.

These three elements should illustrate the kinds of survival needs required by social structure such as organizations and nations. Some sociologists, as we've seen, have developed rather complex models for understanding what Parsons (1951) called *system imperatives*, but we've gotten in deep enough for present purposes. Now let's explore further into the mechanisms through which such needs are satisfied, a topic we've touched on in the discussion of survival needs.

MECHANISMS FOR SURVIVAL

At the risk of tautology (I plead guilty), I suggest that the one survival need of social structure is "survival mechanisms." This very generalized answer allows us to accommodate the variety of ways that different forms of social structure survive. In exploring these varied mechanisms, we'll see that some of the mechanisms involve other elements of social structure and that some focus more directly on individual humans.

Human Mechanisms

Although Maturana's (1980) work on autopoiesis has focused primarily on biological organisms, he and some colleagues also have explored the role of autopoiesis in society, attempting to make the linkage with human beings. The key is to discover ways the participation of individuals in a group realizes the autopoiesis both of each participating individual and of the group itself. For the most part, however, Maturana attempts to link social systems with human beings as *biological systems,* which is understandable in a biologist. In the discussions below, I explore some of the ways social systems are autopoietically linked with individuals as psychological rather than biological entities.

Let's look, then, at some of the ways survival of individuals is linked with survival of the social structure they participate in. Although we begin with biological survival, we will not deal with individuals as systems of cells and organs.

Biological Survival.   Very commonly, human biological survival becomes linked with the survival of social structure. This linkage is evident in the case of the military, for example. In modern societies, individuals give up the responsibility for personally defending themselves from foreign invaders. Instead we depend on the military to serve the function of national defense. We may be called to serve within the military under certain circumstances, but the society as an entity bears the responsibility for seeing that we are protected.

The police occupy a similar position within modern society. Each of us enjoys substantial protection from those around us by virtue of the role we've assigned to the police. Even during times of widespread lawlessness and police ineffectiveness, it still will seem that things would be even worse without the police.

This assignment of responsibility for our physical well-being offers a powerful incentive for protecting the social structure we've established. Even when the military and/or the police come under heavy criticism, few would call for either to be abandoned altogether. The fear we have about how bad things might be for us as individuals is an important force for the survival of the military and the police.

A similar argument can be (and is) made on behalf of governmental regulatory agencies such as the Food and Drug Administration. When you go to the grocery store, I doubt that you worry a great deal about whether the food you are buying will turn out to be poisonous. If you were to propose eliminating the FDA, however, that fear undoubtedly would be raised as an unbeatable argument in support of the agency's survival. Even when agencies perform badly and calamities result, it is more likely that the agencies will be restructured and given more money than that they will be eliminated.

Our dependence on such agencies means that any threat to the survival of the social structure is a threat to the survival of the individuals who depend on it, or at least think they do. Thus social structure, which has no motive or means to act on its own behalf (concepts that apply only to humans), has an army of humans willing to work for its survival.

Individual Identity. I've already drawn attention to how much of our personal identity is drawn from elements of social structure, such as the informal groups and the organizations we belong to. Try answering the question "Who am I?" without any reference to social structure.

Any references to your name or family ties are meaningful only in that they locate you within the network of social statuses within which you relate to others. Being an American or a Virginian are out. So is being a student, a teacher, or any other occupation. Religious or political affiliations are further instances of your integration within social structure; they hardly distinguish you within it. None of these illuminate what makes you special; they just show how you are the same as other people.

Your race is relatively trivial as a biological matter, though it makes a great deal of difference as social structure. Even your gender, which has definite biological consequences, has an even greater impact on your life in terms of the social structural component. The fact that the first 40 presidents of the United States were all white men has nothing to do with biology or gender, nor is it a coincidence.

I hope these few comments will make it inescapably obvious that your identity—who you think you are and who others think you are as they decide how to treat you—is inextricably interwoven with social structure. When people see that you are a black woman, it powerfully affects how they will deal with you. Tell people you are a Roman Catholic, and that too determines how you will be treated. Telling people you are a numbers-runner for the Mafia will have an equally powerful impact. Notice that none of these identities have any meaning except within the complex social structure we created.

Although you are essentially nobody except for your social structural identifications, notice that you have a very personal stake in the well-being of those structures. If you are Jewish and someone attacks Judaism, you are, to some degree, personally attacked. If you are a graduate of State University, notice how anyone criticizing (or flattering) SU has also established a link with you. That person will have become, to some degree, your friend or your enemy.

I do not mean to suggest that anyone who is associated with any social organization is totally devoted to it. That's clearly not the case, as you can undoubtedly attest to in your own experience. I know that you are associated with some groups and organizations that you dislike and would be happy to disassociate yourself from. All of us have examples of that.

Still, in whatever numbers and to whatever degree individual human beings are personally imbedded in social structure, the survival of that structure is enhanced. Threats to the survival of the social structure are threats to the identity of the individuals so entangled in it.

Individual Self-Interest.   Most simply of all, perhaps, some individuals develop a vested self-interest in the survival of some aspects of social structure. In a monarchy, the members of the ruling family have a vested interest in perpetuating the governmental system, and they can be counted on to work toward its survival. Priests would resist the overthrow of a theocracy, just as generals would favor military rule and work for its perpetuation. Successful capitalists resist the overthrow of capitalism. Self-interest is vested more deeply into social structure than may be immediately evident. It certainly extends well beyond matters of power.

In the United States, drivers are expected to drive on the right-hand side of the road; as you know, the agreement in many other countries is to drive on the left-hand side. The norm of which side to drive on is an example of social structure.

Clearly there is no "correct" side of the road to drive on, except that you should follow local customs. Nonetheless people develop powerful attachments to the norm in their society, some of which are related to self-interest. Imagine some of the adjustments that would be required if we were to change our norm to driving on the left. Automobile manufacturers would have to retool their factories to change where they install steering wheels, instrument panels, gear shifts, turn signals, and so on. Drive-up windows at banks, post offices, and fast-food restaurants would no longer work.

If you have ever driven in a country where the norm is to drive on the left, you know how difficult it is to switch from something so habitual. In 1991, I had the opportunity to take a bus trip into the People's Republic of China. Because I had grown accustomed to left-driving throughout Asia, I was amazed to learn that right-driving is the norm in China. I also was impressed by the number of highway accidents I witnessed. Many of them, I was told, involved Hong Kong truck drivers, whose home norm is to drive on the left. Although I've found that I can adapt fairly well to driving on the left-hand side of the road in light traffic, all my instincts in an emergency shift to the right-hand side.

The fact that millions of individuals have become accustomed to driving on a particular side of the road is a powerful force working for the perpetuation of the norm. Once a norm has been established, individuals tend to adjust their lives in accordance with it. Their personal adjustments create a strong incentive for keeping the norm as it is. As long as the norm seems to be working reasonably well, it just seems easier to keep it as it is.

Language is another good example of humans becoming adapted to social structure, with their adaptation becoming a mighty force for its survival. Because I've learned to speak and write English fairly well (I wasn't born that way), I have a real commitment to its perpetuation. Even though it's not politically correct to say so, I admit that I'd be happy to see English adopted as the global language, and I've personally benefitted from the extent to which it already has spread around the globe.

Each of these examples illustrates a common process. Some element of social structure is established. Individuals adapt themselves to it, and, to the extent that they are successful in their adaptation, they are committed to its perpetuation. Notice how nearly automatic this relationship is: If people benefit from an element of social structure, they are likely to support its perpetuation.

Now consider another aspect of the process. People who are generally successful in dealing within the social structure around them are also more likely to achieve positions that will give them more say in whether the social structure is perpetuated or changed. In the case of language, for example, those who are articulate in English are more likely to win political office in America, and they are the ones who will decide whether English remains the dominant language.

Similarly those who are successful capitalists will have the money necessary to ensure the perpetuation of capitalism. Those who have suffered more than they have benefitted from the system will, by that very fact, lack the resources that would be needed to mount a successful movement to change the system.

These, then, are a few of the mechanisms through which social structure is perpetuated. So far, we've been elaborating on the autopoietic quality of social structure: how it is designed to create and re-create itself through its links to the humans involved. Some survival mechanisms don't even have to rely on human motivations. They can be built into the social structure itself.

Social Structural Mechanisms

Officially Mandated Survival. Often the survival of social structure is ordered specifically by the agreements of creation. In any corporation, the board of directors is the legal embodiment of that organization. Even though the staff are more visible to those doing business with the corporation, the directors are the most fundamental members. Even if all of the staff were fired, the corporation still would exist as a legal entity if the board of directors still existed. The articles of incorporation specify the manner in which the board perpetuates itself, indicating how and when new directors will be selected. The leadership of the board is similarly specified through articles spelling out the duties of the officers of the board and the manner in which they are to be selected.

The point is that if the board simply continues to do what its official rules specify, the corporation will be perpetuated. But what if the board simply decided not to follow the rules? Either the corporation's own articles of incorporation or the larger context of corporate law in the society prescribe the sanctions that may befall directors who do not follow such rules. And a part of their punishment would include being replaced by new directors who would follow the rules. Thus it is possible to establish a set of rules that go a good distance toward guaranteeing the perpetuation of social structure.

Institutional Linkages. Sociologists often talk about social integration, meaning the extent to which various elements of social structure are mutually supportive. Although the common tendency is to regard such integration as positive, it is not necessarily so, as we will see.

Think for a moment about some of the ways politics and economics are related in American society. Businesses, for example, generate wealth and pay taxes to government; moreover, they pay wages to workers who pay taxes to government; in fact, the businesses collect the taxes from workers (withholding) on behalf of the government. Government, on the other hand, passes laws that facilitate the operations of business firms, low-interest loans to businesses may be made possible by governmental guarantees, and government may provide funding for training programs to provide the skilled workers needed by businesses.

Or consider a less benign form of mutual support. Candidates for political office receive campaign contributions from businesses that later may expect legislation to support their activities—perhaps at the expense of businesses that did not contribute. This system of mutual support has provided countless scandals during American political history, but for our present purposes, it is more important to recognize the social process at work, rather than the activities of specific individuals. As a process, it describes an aspect of how politics and economics are interwoven in American society.

Although we've only touched on the tiniest faction of possible examples of the interrelationship of politics to economy, let's note some of the ways another institution—say, education—is brought into the system. Government, for example, provides the funding for public education and, through scholarships and research grants, provides major funding for private education as well. On the one hand, the economy, in linking jobs with training, provides a powerful incentive for people to go to school. On the other hand, the schools train people to do the jobs available in the economy. And the schools also teach students about American democracy and instill a respect, even reverence, for such a system.

Notice that these kinds of social structural mechanisms for survival are vulnerable in the same way: Humans created them, and humans can change them. As we will see next, however, humans are woven into the survival of social structure in numerous ways so that they will not make the changes just mentioned. Typically the humans don't want to make the changes. Let's see why.

THE RELATIONSHIP BETWEEN INDIVIDUALS AND SOCIETY

If you were to write an analysis on the rise of Bolshevism in Russia in the early 20th century, you would want to include as causal variables the grinding poverty of the peasants, the insensitivity of the Romanov czars, the brutal oppression of the Cossack soldiers, environmental factors such as periodic famines, and external philosophical ideas such as Marxism. Stir together factors such as these, bring to a boil, and you eventually will generate a combustion. It could happen almost anywhere, as the pressure building up moved from location to location throughout the beleaguered society. As it turns out in this case, it came to a head in the form of *Vladimir Ilyich Lenin*. It is instructive that this well-known name in history is a pseudonym, taken on around 1900 by the son of a school inspector named Ulyanov. I would like to suggest that you consider an unusual point of view for analyzing these matters: that Lenin could have "happened" to anyone. If it hadn't happened to young Ulyanov, it would have happened somewhere else, to someone else—perhaps to Plekhanov, Trotsky, Kerensky, or one of the other early figures in the Russian Revolution. (Perhaps it would have been Pitirim A. Sorokin, an early figure in the revolution, who later became a famous sociologist in the United States.) What "happened" was leadership, and it could have happened to anyone. We might take the point of view that social circumstances generated Lenin, rather than one man's leadership generating the events of history.

I know this is a radically different way of looking at familiar events, and I want to be clear that I am not arguing that it "really" happened that way. Indeed the list of what "really" happened might include such things as

- Vladimir Ulyanov was born in 1874 in the Volga region of Russia.

- His brother, Aleksandr, was executed in 1887 for his role in a plot to assassinate the czar.

- Karl Marx and Friedrich Engels published *The Communist Manifesto* in 1848.

- The Russo-Japanese War of 1904-1905 revealed some of the corruption that had developed in the czarist government.

- In January 1905, a peaceful group of peasants, led by a priest, marched to the winter palace to petition Czar Nicholas II for relief to their suffering; they were fired on by the soldier guarding the palace.

- World War I, beginning in 1914, brought turmoil and the possibility of change to societies throughout Europe.

How all of these ingredients "caused" the Russian Revolution is a matter of interpretation. A common explanation is that all of these factors were brought to a head by the leadership of V. I. Lenin in October 1917. In earlier, more sexist times, scholars referred to such explanations as the "great man" theory of history. Even then, it was only a "theory" and was only one mode of explanation among many. Taking a systems point of view yields a much different explanation.

Just as a biographer might trace the steps in Ulyanov-Lenin's life, showing how each step made sense for a human being experiencing life's events and choosing among its alternatives, we could just as easily focus on the logic by which whole societies operate. Here's a specific example of what I mean.

Earlier I mentioned the violent suppression and massacre of the peasants in 1905 Russia. Following that brutal event and months of civil disorder, Czar Nicholas II gave in to the public demand for political reform. Some basic civil liberties were granted to citizens, and a parliament (Duma) was established. The first Duma, in 1906, and the second, in 1907, however, were dissolved by the czar because he believed they were too hostile to his regime. That belief also resulted in a reinstatement of the government's suppression of dissent.

Some social scientists have been particularly interested in the impact of such waffling on the part of governments. Crane Brinton (1953), for example, introduced the notion of "the revolution of rising expectations." His research into historical events such as the French and Russian revolutions pointed to a common pattern: Uprisings are less common in situations of constant suppression than they are when freedom is first given and then taken away. The initial granting of freedom generates happy expectations for the future; when those expectations are later frustrated, a volatile situation results. Thousands of miles and several decades from the Russian Revolution, the same explanatory model sheds light on the Berkeley student revolt, which began as the free speech movement in the fall of 1964 and spread across the nation.

During a volatile election year—Johnson and Goldwater offered competing views about how to handle the threat of full-scale war in Vietnam, and a variety of civil rights issues touched deep emotions on both the Right and the Left—the University of California's administration initially allowed students to promote various political causes at card tables set up at the Telegraph Avenue entrance to the campus. Quickly this widened strip of sidewalk became the most exciting area of the campus.

As the fall semester got into full swing, the extent of political activity increased dramatically. Although it represented a broad range from Left to Right, the preponderant emphasis was radical Left. This focus began to attract criticism from conservatives in the community and in government. Finally, under the mounting pressure from outside, the administration reconsidered its policy and told students to disband. When some students refused, police were brought on campus to suppress the resistance. As demonstrator Jack Wineberg was escorted into a police car in front of Sproul Hall, adjacent to the scene of political activity, students spontaneously sat down in front of and behind the car, preventing it from leaving campus. By nightfall, 2,000-3,000 students were sitting around the car, and its roof was being used as a stage for a series of speakers. One of the speakers, Mario Savio, became recognized as the chief "leader" of the movement, though he often gave indications of being surprised and perplexed by that turn of events.

Although it is possible to point to the parts played by specific individuals, such as Savio, Wineberg, UC President Clark Kerr, and

Alameda County deputy district attorney Edwin Meese (who later would become President Ronald Reagan's Attorney General), the process of revolt being generated by the frustration of rising expectations has been worked out over and over in countless different times and places. Sometimes the rising expectations involve liberty, sometimes economic prosperity. In either case, there appears to be a process of historical unfolding that supersedes the individual human beings who live through it and are its visible participants.

In this chapter, we've seen that the persistent features of a society—the organizations, institutions, and other elements of social structure—also can be seen as having a "life of their own." Indeed social structure survives only when it is constructed with autopoietic mechanisms for self-creation. The functioning of those mechanisms, then, has a powerful impact in shaping our lives—yours and mine. If you were my student and I your teacher, many of my actions toward you simply could not be explained as a function of my character or personal aspirations, but they would make perfect sense when seen as mechanisms by which a university perpetuates itself. There is an old joke to the effect that a chicken is simply an egg's way of producing more eggs. By the same token, you might say that human beings are merely the vehicle through which social structure perpetuates itself. I know this may seem a bizarre way to think, but it can offer a powerful approach to understanding the interactions between individuals and society. It requires an ability and willingness to see events in unusual and even strange ways, but the insights that can result are both fascinating and useful.

I end this chapter with a paradox that we pursue in later chapters. On the one hand, I hope you have come to appreciate the reality of social structure and the impact it has on all aspects of your life, even if you are unwilling to see yourself as the way society survives. By now, you should at least recognize that, without reference to your place in society, you would not exist as anything remotely resembling who and what you think you are.

And yet, on the other hand, it can be argued with equally compelling logic that social structure does not exist without us. Buckminster Fuller, one of the greatest geniuses of the 20th century, was fond of reminding us that organizations can't act: General Motors can't act, the United States can't act. Only individuals within them can act. Even when we acknowledge the autopoietic and other systemic processes that shape the actions individuals take, it ultimately comes down to individual human beings. Even when social structure seems to shape the decisions you and I make, *we* are the ones who make those decisions.

CONCLUSION

Social structure has an autopoietic quality: It is designed to perpetuate itself. Those elements of social structure that lack survival mechanisms don't survive. We have seen that you and I are often the survival mechanisms for the organizations we belong to, for the norms and values we accept and abide by. In addition, we've seen that survival mechanisms sometimes are built in consciously, like the provisions for replacing members of a board of directors.

Now that we have looked into the tenacity that social structure has for survival, let's look a little more deeply into exactly what it is that survives. That's the task of Chapter 5.

Points of Discussion

- Identify some of the autopoietic aspects of an organization you belong to—those aspects of the organization that have the primary function of keeping the organization in existence.

- What two or more organizations can you think of that have been structured to support each other's survival?

- What are some examples of the survival needs of an organization conflicting with its "official" purpose?

Reading Further

The concept of *autopoiesis* is just starting to become well known in sociology, so the sociological literature on it is not full. The original works on the concept are by two Chilean biologists, Humberto R. Maturana and Francisco J. Varela. Their main thesis is laid out in *Autopoiesis and Cognition* (Dodrecht, Netherlands: Reidel, 1980). It is important to remember that their main focus is on the autopoietic quality of living, biological organisms, although they recognize that this powerful concept has broader applications.

For a more direct look at autopoiesis in a social context, you might consider *Autopoiesis, Communication, and Society,* a book edited by Frank Benseler, Peter M. Heji, and Wolfram K. Kock (Frankfurt, Germany: Campus Verlag, 1980). This book brings together papers presented at a

1979 conference on autopoiesis and its application to such fields as medicine, law, and communications.

Another collection of conference papers, edited by H. Ulrich and G. J. B. Probst, is *Self-Organization and Management of Social Systems* (New York: Springer-Verlag, 1984). Although few of the contributors are social scientists, they direct their attention to the application of autopoietic principles to social systems—especially to the topic of organizational management.

Much of the writing on autopoiesis to date is a bit daunting, especially when written by physicists and biologists intent on applying physical science models to society. However, Gareth Morgan, in *Images of Organization* (Beverly Hills, CA: Sage, 1986) provides a more readable discussion of the topic in his examination of "organizations as brains" (Chapter 4), relating autopoiesis to cybernetics, holographics, and other mind-bending concepts.

CHAPTER FIVE

What Exactly Survives?

Organizations and other forms of social structure have the quality of persisting over time. That's obvious to anyone. What's not obvious is precisely what it is that persists. That is the question we address in this chapter.

I am 54 years old as I write this, and I have a problem about that. I don't mind being that old, but it annoys me that I can't say exactly *what* it is that's 54 years old. This is a problem that first troubled me a few years ago when I began exploring the notion of self-concept and, more to the point, self. None of the likely answers to that question work for me. This body isn't 54 years old; it didn't look anything like this when I was born. As far as I know, I looked like all babies, and I was certainly a lot smaller than this. Moreover, I'm told that my cells will have totally replaced themselves every 7 years or so.

Because I was born Earl Eugene Arbuckle, my name isn't 54 years old. My memories keep changing, and so does my personality (to some degree at least), so none of that is what's 54 years old. I've told you about this problem of personal identity as a way of introducing the topic of this chapter. We face a similar problem when we speak of the survival of social structure. When we say that a norm, value, organization, or society survives, what is it exactly that survives?

To get into this question, let's look at a case study of a concrete organization that has survived over time. As we look more deeply into the matter, however, the question of *what* survived becomes more and more elusive.

THE HISTORY OF A COLLEGE HISTORY

In 1991, Chapman College, a medium-sized liberal arts college in Orange, California, became Chapman University and celebrated 130 years of commitment to higher education. That's the sort of event treasured by many organizations, as it offers a time for reflection and celebration.

For purposes of our present examination, the question is: If Chapman University was 130 years old in 1991, *what exactly was it that was 130 years old?* It is easy to point to some of the things that were *not* 130 years old. Certainly none of the students, professors, staff, or administrators had lasted through that history. Moreover, the 1991 university catalog points out that neither the name nor the location has persisted for 130 years.

The Hesperian Roots

In the university catalog for the 1991-92 academic year, Chapman's history is described as follows:

> Chapman traces its roots to Hesperian College, founded at the very hour of Abraham Lincoln's inauguration as the sixteenth U.S. president. Hesperian and several other institutions later merged with California Christian College in Los Angeles. In 1934 the institution was renamed in recognition of its most generous benefactor, C. C. Chapman, successful real estate investor, rancher and pioneer Orange County church leader. The college moved to the city of Orange in 1954. In September of 1991 the college became Chapman University, further strengthening its commitment to graduate programs, international education and an innovative undergraduate curriculum. (Chapman University, 1991, p. 17)

The origins of Hesperian College are detailed in Haworth Alfred Clover's 1960 master's thesis. Clover quotes from a Woodland newspaper:

> The opening of the new Hesperian College building took place today at 10:30 a.m. The Chapel basement was well filled with pupils, professors, friends, and visitors. The opening exercises were commenced with general singing, led by Miss Josie Watkins as organist. After which Professor Elston, President of the College, made a short speech upon "Knowledge is Power" which he concluded by referring to the knowledge of the Bible, which lay open before him, as the foundation and true source of all knowledge and power. (Clover, 1960, p. 198)

Clover's account indicates that the founders of Hesperian College chose the opening date very consciously, correctly believing it to be an auspicious date in history. In fact, to coincide with Abraham Lincoln's inauguration as president of the United States, the school officially began instruction a few days before its main building was finished. If Hesperian College were in existence today, probably no one would dispute the claim of being 130 years of age in 1991. But what does it mean that Chapman "traces its roots to Hesperian College," as described in the 1991-92 catalog? And if Chapman could be said to be 130 years old, what is it exactly that was 130 years old?

A slightly earlier (1985-86) catalog tells a similar story of Chapman's roots; it offers a bit more concrete data about the 1934 name change and the 1954 move from Los Angeles to Orange, but it is also somewhat ambiguous about the Hesperian roots:

> Chapman College is named in honor of Charles C. Chapman (1853-1944), pioneer Orange County church leader, real estate investor, and rancher. In the early years of this century Mr. Chapman was the leader among members of the Christian Churches of Southern California in founding a four-year liberal arts college (California Christian College, incorporated in 1918). He remained a vital force in the growth of the College until his death, giving his time and resources to further the cause of higher education for Christian leadership. In 1934 the institution's name was changed to Chapman College by unanimous vote of the Board of Trustees.
>
> Chapman is part of a long heritage of higher education in California related to the Christian Church (Disciples of Christ), dating back to Hesperian College, founded by members of the Christian Church in Woodland on March 4, 1861. This institution and several others later merged with California Christian College in Los Angeles. Thus, Chapman is the legal, educational, and spiritual successor of Hesperian College.
>
> In 1954 the College was moved from Los Angeles to the present campus in Orange, providing the benefits of life in a smaller community and improved plant facilities. Chapman is committed by its Board of Trustees to a comprehensive program of growth and improvement. (Chapman College, 1985, p. 3)

This statement mentions that Hesperian College and "several others" merged before moving to Los Angeles. The others referred to are Pierce Christian College and Christian College at Santa Rosa. In 1896, the three merged and formed the Berkeley Bible Seminary, moving to the city of that name. Shortly after, BBS moved across the bay to San Francisco, where it stayed until 1920.

While discussing the change of name and the physical relocation, the 1985-86 catalog suggests Chapman is the "legal, educational, and spiritual successor to Hesperian College." Therein lies the claim of a 130-year history for Chapman. But what exactly does it mean?

Or Did It All Begin in 1920?

As we move back through the college catalogs, the same history is repeated, always stressing the continuity of the college despite the changes of location and name. The 1942-43 catalog account of college history, however, is quite different. It begins:

> The foundations of the college were laid in the deep desire of the Disciples of Christ in California to create an institution of Christian learning to serve not their own educational needs alone, but the general cause of Christian culture.
>
> In 1912 Mr. Charles C. Chapman pledged, for the starting of a new college, $50,000, upon the condition that the Disciples of Christ in California secure an additional $150,000. In 1919 Mr. Chapman declared his intention of giving $200,000, provided his brethren in the churches of Southern California would raise an additional $100,000. (Chapman College, 1942, p. ix)

The account goes on to acknowledge the other major contributors, as well as Mr. Chapman's subsequent doubling of his challenge pledge. The final paragraph begins: "The work of instruction was begun September 13, 1920, in temporary quarters in the Wilshire Boulevard Christian Church" (Chapman College, 1942, p. ix).

Nowhere in the account is there any mention of Hesperian College and its 1861 creation during Abraham Lincoln's inauguration! The same historical account, moreover, appears in all of the catalogs from 1936-37 through 1942-43.

The very first (1921-22) catalog of California School of Christianity describes the same Hesperian-less history, though with more details about the early fund-raising activities. The "Historical Sketch" began:

> The vision of a great institution of learning to serve the Christian Churches of California, as an educational, evangelizing and spiritual center, was first proposed at a great brotherhood meeting in Los Angeles in 1909. This was followed by the appointment of an Educational Committee by the Christian Ministers' Association of Southern California to pioneer the way. (California School of Christianity, 1921, p. 7)

The committee brought a proposal for establishing a college to the church's state convention in 1912. After a brief discussion on the report,

Charles C. Chapman, president of the convention, called on a clergyman to lead a prayer for divine guidance.

> A hush and reverence fell upon all as this heartfelt petition was made. The resolution was then unanimously approved. Then, at this critical moment President Chapman voiced the deep conviction of all present. He said: "This movement is plainly of Divine leading; we dare not pause or turn back; the movement must go forward at once; I therefore now offer $50,000.00 to this cause conditioned upon the churches raising an additional $150,000.00." The convention at once broke into hearty applause, and rose spontaneously and sang the Doxology. (California School of Christianity, 1921, p. 7)

The historical sketch in the 1921-22 catalog continues to describe the successful fund-raising campaign, including the 1919 convention at which Chapman raised his personal pledge from $50,000 to $200,000. (The convention again arose spontaneously and sang the Doxology.)

The 1921-22 catalog also discusses the nature of the link between the Berkeley Bible Seminary and what was to become Chapman.

> Following the convention the brethren in California North were invited to join in the enterprise, adding the assets of Berkeley Bible Seminary to the funds in the South and, merging that school with the new institution, present to the brotherhood of the state one institution of learning for the training of our young people, and which by reason of united support, might be developed into a first-class institution. These overtures were kindly received by the brethren in Northern California, and, on April 7, 1920, the consolidation of "California Bible College" [sic] and "California Christian College" was effected under the name "California School of Christianity," with the trustees of the two institutions forming the new board, as provided by law. (California School of Christianity, 1921, p. 8)

The 1922-23 catalog lists the trustees of the combined college and indicates 13 were from Los Angeles and Orange County and 8 were from Northern California. However, in a conversation with Irvin Chapman, son of C. C. Chapman, and a college trustee since 1936, I was told that the northern trustees never really participated because of their distance (prior to jet travel and freeways) from the college. Chapman also indicated that no students came south with the transfer, although the Dean of the Berkeley Bible Seminary did move and served as one of the first two professors at the California School of Christianity. The BBS library and other assets, totaling an estimated $50,000, were also a part of the merger.

To recap, then, Charles Chapman and his co-religionists clearly believed they were establishing a new college in Southern California between 1912 and 1920. The initiative was their own; they raised the money needed to create the new school. Near the end of their efforts, they invited the struggling Berkeley Bible Seminary to transfer its assets to the new venture. This perception of what happened is quite different from the idea that the Berkeley Bible Seminary (a.k.a. Hesperian College) moved to Los Angeles and changed its name to the California School of Christianity.

In support of the idea of persistence is the transfer of $50,000, an unknown number of books, and a former dean. Arguing against the survival of the earlier colleges is the independent efforts of the southern Disciples, their greater financial contribution, and the lack of students bridging the gap between BBS and CSC.

Another possible thread of continuity, however, is mission. The 1909 convention set its goal as establishing "an educational, evangelizing and spiritual center"—the same basic mission that produced Hesperian College in 1861. We can only assume that the northern Disciples felt that joining with a new venture in Los Angeles would forward their own mission.

It is worth noting that, initially, the California School of Christianity primarily offered courses in religion. Secular courses were taken from the University of California, Southern Branch (now UCLA), located just across the street from the Vermont Street campus of CSC,

> because of the facilities afforded by the State University for thorough instruction in all secular branches, without cost to our own institution; allowing the latter to use its own equipment and faculty for purposes of distinctively moral and religious education, thus accomplishing vastly larger and more effective results than would be possible, were we required to supply the entire curriculum for the student body. (California School of Christianity, 1921, p. 13)

In December 1921, however, the CSC board of trustees voted to expand the offerings of the college.

There is a fundamental problem, however, with basing the argument of organizational survival on the matter of mission. No one would suggest that the contemporary university is devoted to the same mission as either Hesperian College or the California School of Christianity. Although Chapman still maintains loose connections with the Disciples of Christ, it is hardly a "church school." Moreover, only 6-7% of the contemporary student body are members of the Disciples. By contrast, about a quarter are Roman Catholic, and one in six students claims no religious affiliation at all.

In summary, the question of whether the California School of Christianity, renamed in 1921 as the California Christian College, was a new school or merely the continued evolution of Hesperian College is, at best, ambiguous. The 1945-46 Chapman catalog, however, seems quite clear in the matter. "The college [Berkeley Bible Seminary] was moved to Los Angeles in the fall of 1920 and during that year was known as the California School of Christianity" (p. 6). Although this quote is not altogether incorrect, it is somewhat akin to saying that in 1960, Hawaii was renamed and began doing business as the United States of America.

The View From Los Angeles

Early documents proffer no sense of organizational continuity in the California Christian College. The May 1927 *California Christian Collegian,* for example, announced: "The fifth annual commencement program will take place in Grayson Memorial Auditorium on Thursday, June 9th, at ten o'clock" (p. 6).

Along the same lines, the June 1928 edition of the *California Christian Collegian* declared: "Once again we can truthfully say, this is our largest class to be graduated. It is the sixth" (p. 2). The commencement announcement for 1929 read: "The Trustees and Faculty invite you to attend the Seventh Annual Commencement Exercises June 9-14, 1929."

In June 1930, the *California Christian Collegian* ran news of the commencement under the headline: "EIGHTH GRADUATING CLASS IS LARGEST, NUMBERING 20" (p. 1). It went on to elaborate: "The decade year of California Christian College is fittingly the eighth and largest graduating class, numbering five women and fifteen men, twenty in all" (p. 1).

Thus there is ample evidence that those associated with Chapman during the 1920s believed they were the founding pioneers of a new college. Here's what students wrote in the 1923 yearbook, *CEER.*

> Memory carries us back to the thirteenth day of September, 1920, when ten of us met as the first Student Body, at the Wilshire Blvd. Christian Church. It is hard to say just what our thoughts and hopes were at that time, but all had supreme confidence in the new institution that was to train young people to do more effective Christian work. These ten students realized that they were to be the foundation upon which a larger and more adequate institution must build, and so with that in mind they,

in co-operation with the faculty, which at that time consisted of two members only, set to work to build a standard that would be worthy of following.

Footnote: By the second year, 1921-22, the faculty had doubled to four: three religion professors and one *sociology* professor! (California School of Christianity, 1923, p. 17)

The perception of Chapman history shifted significantly between 1942 and 1944, with the result that its origins receded from the California School of Christianity of 1920 Los Angeles to Hesperian College of 1861 Woodland. The shift in views of Chapman's pedigree appears to have taken place in the midst of a serious crisis of continuity.

The Whittier Hiatus

The year 1942 represents a serious disjuncture in the life of Chapman College. The exigencies of World War II and financial problems at the college resulted in Chapman giving its campus to the military for training purposes. The college moved its activities to the nearby Whittier College campus. The 1946-47 catalog relates the history of the time thusly:

> In the year 1942, Chapman College entered into a temporary cooperative educational program with Whittier College. The terms of this cooperative program were made necessary by the war emergency; during these years the Vermont Avenue campus was used by both the Army and the Navy. Circumstances now permit Chapman College to return to its own campus and a new educational program is being inaugurated. (Chapman College, 1946, p. 6)

The assertion that Chapman College continued through the Whittier years is challenged by Paul S. Delp, a member of the California Christian College class of 1928, also listed as a Chapman philosophy professor in the 1941-42 catalog. Now an honored professor emeritus at Chapman University, Delp still recalls the remarkable transformation clearly today. When I interviewed him on October 11, 1991, he described the events of that period as follows:

> Cecil Cheverton was the president of the college in 1942, and we were having financial difficulties. Cheverton had been negotiating with Occidental College on the possibility of a merger. Then, at the final faculty meeting of the Spring of 1942, there was a knock at the door and in walked George Reeves, a local pastor and member of the college's Board of Trustees.

Reeves announced that we were being terminated and that the college was being moved temporarily to the Whittier campus. We were all shocked, as you can imagine, and it was doubly upsetting soon after to learn that Dr. Cheverton had suffered a nervous breakdown. Then we discovered that George Reeves was the new president of Chapman.

The students were so upset by the changes that it was mostly just the senior class who made the move to Whittier with Reeves; they wanted to graduate. Few of the other students made the move. Soon Chapman had virtually no students of its own, although Reeves began claiming Whittier's 400 students as belonging to Chapman.

When Chapman left Whittier at the end of the war, it had to begin recruiting a new student body and a new faculty from scratch. In a real sense, Chapman College went out of existence during the war years.

And when Reeves restarted the college again afterward, he created the myth that Chapman could be traced all the way back to Lincoln. (P. S. Delp, personal communication, October 11, 1991)

There is ample evidence that the move to Whittier raised serious concerns among students and alumni about the survival of the college. President Reeves also sought to allay those concerns with an article in the September 1, 1942, *Chapman College Alumnus* (Reeves, 1942). As Reeves, sounding much like today's political "spin doctors," explained,

The college is happily located for the present on Whittier College campus. The arrangement can be quickly summarized in this way: Whittier provides its full academic program, and Chapman provides its full religious program to a common curriculum open to all students. By this arrangement, there have been made available to Chapman students more than twice as many courses as have been open to them previously. And yet at the same time the college budget will be kept within the college income. (pp. 1, 4)

Although the Chapman administration remained separate from Whittier's, is that sufficient to say that *Chapman College* had survived and, if so, what exactly was it that survived? How about the faculty, for example?

The 1941-42, pre-Whittier, Chapman catalog listed 19 faculty members, including Professor Delp. No 1943-44 catalog is on file in the Chapman library, but the 1944-45 catalog lists a combined Whittier-Chapman faculty of 43 members, roughly corresponding to Reeves's claim that the number of courses available to students was roughly double what it had been prior to the move. A careful review of the two faculty lists in question indicates that none of the 1941-42 Chapman faculty made the move.

The only continuity from Chapman to Whittier-Chapman would appear to be President Reeves and Dean Rush Deskins. The latter did not appear in the 1941-42 Chapman catalog, but the 1944 *CEER* identifies him as having been "dean of the college since 1942."

Dean Deskins's statement in that yearbook addressed the difficulty of the move and presented his own, rather dramatic view of the college's organizational survival.

> The three years I have taught in our college have been the most tragic years of its history. Soon after my coming one could see the clouds of adversity gathering. I sat through many meetings where one could almost hear the solemn dirge of death. During the three intervening years I have discovered a certain invincible spirit that shall never know defeat. It gives one the assurance that Chapman's brightest days are ahead. A small band of students had drunk deeply of that spirit. I have sat through meetings with them and heard them weep for their Alma Mater and her ideals. I have sat through a number of meetings of her Board of Trustees and the same invincible spirit was there. It is the same spirit that came off victorious from Calvary. Christ came down from the cross to live in people and institutions. He is in Chapman College. Therefore, out of three years of darkness the dawn of a new day of victory is appearing in the east, for a brotherhood has caught the spirit and is saying "Shall not perish from the earth." Victorious, we hail thee. (Deskins, 1944, p. 21)

The 1942-43 Chapman catalog is essentially the Whittier catalog, with some introductory notes about Chapman. The course listings for religion, however, indicate two Whittier faculty and three from Chapman: George N. Reeves, Rush M. Deskins, and Royal J. Dye. (Dye's primary work was off-campus, though he sometimes taught.) In the 1944-45 catalog, Bert C. Williams joined as a fourth Chapman faculty member in religion. For all intents and purposes, however, Chapman students were taught by Whittier faculty during the war years.

If the faculty did not provide the continuity for organizational survival, how about the student body? Unlike the 1920 shift from BBS to CSC, a sizable Chapman student body made the move to the Whittier campus. For the most part, however, it was not a happy move from the students' standpoint. There are numerous indications of the anguish accompanying the Whittier years. In part, these were not good years for enrollments. The total numbers of students enrolled are not available, but the 1987 *Alumni Directory* indicates the number graduating each year.

Table 5.1. Number of Students Graduating From Chapman, 1920-1950.

1920: 1	1931: 33	1941: 58
1922: 2	1932: 40	1942: 59
1923: 5	1933: 28	**1943: 31 (Whittier)**
1924: 8	1934: 45	**1944: 20 (Whittier)**
1925: 11	1935: 41	**1945: 12 (Whittier)**
1926: 14	1936: 48	1946: 16
1927: 18	1937: 34	1947: 37
1928: 22	1938: 38	1948: 39
1929: 18	1939: 49	1949: 55
1930: 18	1940: 50	1950: 80

SOURCE: *Data are from the 1987 Alumni Directory of Chapman College, Orange, CA.*

Table 5.1 shows the initial, fairly steady growth of the college and a disastrous plunge during the Whittier years, followed by a subsequent recovery.

Moreover, evidence indicates that the students were actively concerned over the problem of Chapman's identity as a separate entity during the Whittier years. The March 1943 *Chapman College Review* was mostly devoted to the story "Sixty Students in Search of a Campus," which dominated the front page and continued throughout the magazine. Beneath the striking headline was a picture of the Chapman students, who seemed to be writing primarily to potential donors when they said, "We are appealing to all of you who are interested in the continuation of Chapman College to help us in building our school once more" (p. 1).

The appeal focused directly on the sense of college continuity and survival. Freshmen among the article's authors said, "We, as freshmen, know very little of the Chapman traditions or ideals because the Whittier atmosphere is prevalent everywhere. Our friends are in Whittier as well as in Chapman. Therefore, we are torn between two schools" ("Sixty Students," 1943, p. 3).

A sophomore wrote, "We will soon be the last students who were actually a part of the Chapman of memories. We are the ones who must pass on this vital part of Chapman College" (p. 4). These two students state the issue of social structural survival about as clearly as is possible, represented in the sophomore's reference to "this vital part of Chapman College."

There is no doubt that the war years represented a serious identity crisis for Chapman, severely threatening its organizational survival. There is reason to believe, moreover, that President Reeves created the idea of Chapman originating in 1861, perhaps in response to that crisis of continuity and perhaps also as a fund-raising device.

A Surprise Birthday Party

The final page of the August 1943 issue of the *Chapman College Review* carried the following request of readers, under the headline "Data Needed for Historical File."

> Those friends of Christian education who remember the colleges in the west that preceded Chapman College will be interested to know that an historical file has been created and is being maintained to collect information on the colleges and churches of the states of California, Nevada, Arizona and Utah. Due to the fact that Chapman College is the only agency of the Christian Church that represents all of the Christian churches in this four-state area, it has been felt that it would be of great service to establish this historical file of material relating to the total information in this territory.
>
> Anyone having accurate information regarding Hesperian College, Pierce College, Christian College at Santa Rosa, Berkeley Bible Seminary or any other materials relating to other colleges or church schools or history of our churches is invited to see that that information is sent to Chapman College Library, where all information will be carefully filed for future reference for the use of students or others who might be interested. ("Data Needed," 1943, p. 4)

The historical files paid a dividend later that year, when President Reeves began his "President's Message" in the December 1943 *Chapman College Review* as follows:

> Dear Friends:
>
> There are three things of especial interest that have come to the front this past month; and, I believe, you will be as interested in them as I am. The first is the successful completion of our search for the authentic date regarding the history of Chapman College. Many people thought that Chapman College went back only to the year 1919-20, when, as a matter of fact, it will soon be eighty-three years old. (p. 2)

Following a historical account taking Hesperian through the Berkeley Bible Seminary and south to California Christian College, Reeves concluded: "Thus, Chapman College is, by authentic legal record, one of the oldest educational institutions of collegiate grade in the State of California" (p. 2).

President Reeves wasted no time in acting on his amazing discovery. In the March 1944 *Chapman College Review,* Reeves reminded readers of Lincoln's historic inauguration on March 4, 1861, and, in that context, reported on his efforts to raise the funds needed to create a new campus for Chapman:

> For it was on that date, March 4, 1861, that Hesperian College opened its doors and classes assembled for the first time in this educational experiment which today is known as Chapman College. . . .
>
> For seven weeks we have been engaged in a campaign to determine whether that historic institution begun on March 4, 1861, shall pay off its indebtedness and live, or whether it shall "perish from the earth." ("President's Message," 1944, p. 2)

Reeves was successful in his fund-raising activities, and Chapman was able to leave Whittier and move into new quarters at 766 North Vermont Street in Los Angeles. Chapman was once again unquestionably a distinct entity as of September 1945. Its newly ancient history, however, survived the troubled times that generated it. The college's rebirth in history did not take effect right away. Although Reeves had declared as early as December 1943 that Chapman dated from 1861, the commencement announcement of the following spring welcomed people to the 22nd annual commencement, not the 82nd. The next 4 years followed that same view of history. Not until 1950 did the commencement programs catch up with the new past.

1944: Twenty-second Annual Commencement

1945: Twenty-third Annual Commencement

1946: Twenty-fourth Annual Commencement

1947: Twenty-fifth Annual Commencement

1948: Twenty-sixth Annual Commencement

1949: [program missing from files]

1950: Eighty-eighth Annual Commencement

From 1950 forward, Chapman was officially born back in 1861. This development should point to the complexity of the task we set for ourselves in this chapter. (Actually *I* set the task for us, but you came along. You could have said something if you disagreed.)

NOTHING PERSISTS

In Chapter 4, we saw that social structure is autopoietically designed to assure its own survival. Because survival means persistence over time, this chapter has sought to determine what exactly it is that persists. To aid in this inquiry, we have analyzed a specific example: an organization now known as Chapman University.

So when did today's Chapman University begin? Was it in Woodland on March 4, 1861, doing business as Hesperian College? Did it begin in 1896 as the Berkeley Bible Seminary or in 1920 as California School of Christianity? Perhaps it really began in 1934 with the change of name to Chapman College. There are grounds for arguing the current college really began with its departure from Whittier in September 1945. Others might believe that what we know as Chapman today dates from the 1954 move out of Los Angeles and onto the present campus in Orange. Finally the case could be made that Chapman *University* has existed only since 1991, with its latest name change.

The confusing chronicle of Chapman's history of histories highlights something more fundamental than the specific details of this case. Consider Harvard College by way of contrast. Harvard was chartered in 1636 in Cambridge, Massachusetts. As of 1992, it had been doing business in the same location (and under the same name) for 356 years, but is Harvard really 356 years old? If it is, then we must again ask *What exactly is 356 years old?* None of the people involved in Harvard have survived the years. The campus certainly has changed a great deal, and the library holdings keep growing and changing. The curricula are a source of periodic debate and revision.

When I was young, my favorite baseball team was the Boston Braves; Eddie Matthews, on third base, was my personal idol. In the years since, the Braves moved, first to Milwaukee and then to Atlanta. Eddie Matthews even managed the team for a while in Atlanta. But is it still the same team? Or, more accurately, perhaps, in what way is it the same team?

In another baseball example, Leo Durocher died in 1991, at the age of 86. Controversial manager of several teams during his career, Leo "the Lip" was most remembered for managing the Brooklyn Dodgers from 1938 to 1948. Because Durocher had been retired from baseball for many years at the time of his death, the media had to use some ingenuity to establish an "official" comment on his passing. They went to Los Angeles, 3,000 miles from where Durocher had managed, to get a team comment from people who knew him only by reputation. The Los Angeles Dodgers of the 1990s are hardly the same baseball team as the Brooklyn Dodgers of Durocher's time. Yet there was some sense that the LA Dodgers was "the team Durocher managed."

We could continue this conversation, asking who or what exactly is the Democratic Party? the Roman Catholic Church? IBM? Albania? Each presumably has been around for some time, but what exactly has persisted over time?

I titled this section "Nothing Persists." By that, I mean that no *thing* necessarily persists when social structure survives. We've seen that through the process of elimination in examining Chapman University. If a university is its faculty, then Chapman ceased to exist in the spring of 1942, when all of the faculty were terminated. If a university is its student body, then the Berkeley Bible Seminar died in 1920, and the California School of Christianity was a new, separate entity. If a university is its name, Chapman College began in 1934, Chapman University in 1991. If it is its physical plant, then Chapman began in 1957, with the move to its present location, and presumably dies and is reborn every time a new building is put up or an old one is taken down.

You may recall an earlier discussion in which I suggested to you that social structure was more of a process than a thing. It is a process of organizing people's freedom. I now suggest to you that the process of getting people to surrender some of their freedom and organizing those bits of individual freedom into collective action is what persists. Such a process can be initiated at a specific point in time, and such processes can be designed to perpetuate themselves. Sometimes the processes survive for a long time; sometimes they peter out.

In 1861, members of the Disciples of Christ church initiated a process for gaining parts of people's freedom (e.g., some of their time and money) and focusing those on the collective purpose of higher education. They called their creation Hesperian College. A few years later, other Disciples initiated a similar process that they named Pierce Christian College. A similar process was established as Christian College in Santa Rosa. By 1896, these three separate processes were on the verge of extinction, suffering shortages of students and funds.

In 1896, the three independent processes of gaining and organizing individuals' freedom were brought together and renamed the Berkeley Bible Seminary. It was not unlike the result when three small streams come together to form a river. Whether the resulting river is something new or a continuation of one, two, or three of the original streams is solely a matter of definition. So it was with the Berkeley Bible Seminary. It is clear, however, that the resulting process came from the three ongoing processes; no new entity was created independent of the existing ones.

A different situation occurred in 1920. Disciples in Southern California created a new organizing process: getting and structuring people's time and money. Just as their organizational efforts were coming to a head, the earlier process, then called the Berkeley Bible Seminary, was merged into the new effort. Returning to the river analogy, it was as though a large wellhead were pouring forth a large river and a smaller stream began feeding into it. In this case, the new river would have occurred with or without the smaller stream. Whether the California School of Christianity (later, California Christian College) was a new organization or a continuation of Hesperian College (a.k.a. Berkeley Bible Seminary) is a matter of agreement only. Our review of the early documents makes it clear that those involved in launching the ongoing process in 1920 believed they were starting something new. They did not see themselves as merely joining something already in progress. When the enterprise was renamed Chapman College in 1934, that reconfirmed the earlier view.

We have seen that, between 1942 and 1945, the organizing process now called Chapman College was again in danger of extinction with its move to Whittier College. And as we also have seen, autopoietic processes are designed for their own survival. In this instance, the process survived by redefining its origins, declaring itself to be the oldest college in the West, attaching itself to Abraham Lincoln, and crying out for help lest it "perish from the earth."

Some of the survival mechanisms operating on behalf of the persistence of the organizing process called Chapman College included:

- an administrative staff who would be unemployed if the college died. One of their number, President Reeves, played the central role in the redefinition of origins.
- a board of trustees who drew status from serving on the board of a college and who were associated personally with its success.
- a student body, all identifying themselves, in part, as Chapman students and tying their plans for a college education to Chapman. The death of the college would have required a restructuring of their identities, as well as making new arrangements for a college education.

– an alumni who faced the prospect of being graduates of something that didn't exist. Some of them hotly objected to the redefining of Chapman's roots, however, because that violated their own,
earlier experiences as pioneers in something new.

These mechanisms, and many others, operated successfully in keeping the organizing process alive. In this instance, the survival of the
process did not involve a change of name, though a change of venue
occurred as Chapman got a divorce from Whittier.

It is worth repeating at this point that when I talk about organizing
processes being designed for their own survival and when we see
individual human beings acting on behalf of the survival of those
processes, I do not suggest, nor should you believe, that the processes
are themselves human, godlike, or alien spirits. The organizing processes we call social structure do not have spirits or souls or anything
mysterious like that. Social structure is designed for survival the way
rivers are designed to run downhill.

Perhaps a more useful analogy for you to keep in mind is that of the
automobile. The internal combustion engine is designed to convert the
chemical energy in gasoline into kinetic energy. Thus the car's purpose
is to move from Point A to Point B. It can do that only if gasoline is put
into the tank. The automobile as a system, then, includes the human
beings who use it. When it runs out of gasoline and threatens to give up
its designed function, the larger system is structured to have the humans
involved fill up the tank with gasoline.

Notice that the automobile does not have a spirit or a soul or anything
like that. It does not have a "will to go" anymore than social structure
has a "will to live." It simply has been designed so that the humans who
think they can profit from the car's functioning are motivated to ensure
its proper operation.

Human beings construct social structure of all kinds. Sometimes we
do it with specific purposes in mind (creating a factory to make widgets).
Sometimes we create social structure unconsciously or unintentionally,
though we usually can identify some underlying purposes. Thus, for
example, we may come to establish customs or other patterns of social
behavior because they give us a feeling of security. We don't know that's
why we formed the custom, but we've created something on which
our sense of security now depends. When someone strays from tradition, we feel insecure and do what we can to bring the errant member
back into line.

Social structure, in sum, is not a thing; it is an organizing process. As such, it does not have the kind of persistence we associate with things. This means that Harvard is not 356 years old. Chapman is not 130 years old, 71 years old, or even 1 year old. Organizations and other forms of social structure—such as norms, values, beliefs, institutions, and the like—are organizing processes that exist in the present. They are designed for their own survival into the future, and we speak of their existence in the past, but we've seen how difficult it is to pinpoint what survives, because the organizing processes we've examined involve a continuing evolution of all of the tangible material: students, faculty, building, and so forth. Even the purpose for organizing people's freedom can evolve (providing Christian education to providing secular education) while the organizing process itself persists.

A common element in social structure, however, is a *belief* about its age. Although anthropologists have observed various *creation myths* among preliterate societies, we tend to view our creations as a matter of *history*. I suggest, however, that this view reflects mere arrogance or shortsightedness more than ontological or epistemological superiority over our less literate cousins.

The manifestations of social structure exist now and now and now and now . . . and that's it. They are changing all of the time and do not really persist. I make this assertion in the same spirit that Heraclitus noted we can never "step twice into the same river." You cannot attend the same college on two different days, work at the same office, or live in the same marriage. Everything is constantly changing, sometimes imperceptibly, sometimes radically. Often social structures contain beliefs about their origins and history. In fact, such beliefs can have power and are important to the needs of the individuals involved, as well as to the success and survival of the social structure itself. We saw this in the fund-raising potential of Reeves's "discovery" that Chapman was 60 years older than previously believed.

HOW OLD
IS A HUMAN BEING?

I began this chapter with a complaint about not knowing what part of me was 54 years old. The above assertion about the age of social structure might be applied as well to the case of humans. Although we are able to mark our beginnings with the date on our driver's licenses, just as corporations may mark their beginnings with the dates shown on their incorporation papers, what does either mark the beginning of? At best, it is the beginning of an evolving story. Every day, the story is somewhat different.

More interesting than what may or may not actually persist is the belief in persistence. In recent years, some biologists have begun addressing this issue. For example, Milan Zeleny (1981), having noted that the average nerve cell changes its molecular components some 10,000 times during its lifetime, poses a striking question:

> If we now ponder the overall macromolecular and cellular contingent of a human body, and the ceaseless birth, renewal, death and translocation of such components, how do we account for our perception of identity, autonomy and integrity of ourselves? How do we account for the relative stability of our basic patterns of behavior, our personality traits, our memories, our sense of individuality and unity of the whole of our existence? (p. 4)

It was precisely questions such as these, the puzzle of what constitutes life itself, that generated the notion of autopoiesis as a self-creating process. Only now are we beginning to recognize that the same phenomenon accounts for the persistence of society.

CONCLUSION

This chapter began with the question of what persists when social structure survives over time. To pursue an answer to that question, we delved deeply into a specific example: the history of Chapman University. We began with the official assertion that Chapman was 130 years old in 1991 and asked what actually had been around for 130 years.

Through the process of elimination, we found that none of the ordinary manifestations of a college—such as faculty, students, buildings—had survived the 130-year trek. The name, location, and purpose had all changed during that time.

We concluded that social structure is really just an *organizing process*, and an evolving one at that. The matter of age for any of the manifestations of that process is mostly a matter of agreement. In the case of Chapman, moreover, we found that the agreement can change. Thus, from 1920 to 1945, the humans involved in Chapman believed it began in 1920. In 1945, a new creation myth—that Chapman really began in 1861—was put forward and eventually became accepted. There is no answer to the question of how old it really is.

What really persists is the organizing process itself. We've seen that social structure is autopoietically designed to guarantee its own survival.

Social structure is a process of organizing individuals' freedom, and a part of the organization consists of mechanisms that bring the human participants to work for the survival of the organizing process.

This discussion of social structure may have made you somewhat uneasy, feeling that you are trapped in something you previously were unaware of and cannot escape. What you are experiencing is what Max Weber called the "iron cage." Before our investigation is over, you will discover that it is possible to rise above the apparent trap of social structure, that it doesn't have to suppress us. Before we get to that happy outcome, however, we need to look a little more closely into the malfunctioning of social structure.

Points of Discussion

- Who are you? Write 20 answers to this question. How many of them are embedded in social structure?

- Identify experiences in which you were acting on behalf of the survival of social structure.

- In what ways might you say that Chapman University became an entity committed to its own survival? How did that commitment manifest? If possible, name some examples of this phenomenon from your own experience.

Reading Further

Social Institutions: Their Emergence, Maintenance, and Effects, edited by Michael Hechter, Karl-Dieter Opp, and Reinhard Wippler (New York: Aldine, 1990) offers an introduction to the rational choice theory's approach to the rise and development of social institutions.

The Social Fabric, edited by James F. Short, Jr. (Beverly Hills, CA: Sage, 1986) provides a number of articles relevant to a consideration of what persists when social structure survives, such as Mary Douglas's discussion of "Institutionalized Public Memory."

To truly stretch your imagination regarding the nature of social structure and its process, you might enjoy Peter M. Senge's *The Fifth Discipline: The Art and Practice of the Learning Organization* (Garden City, NY: Doubleday, 1990). Director of MIT's Systems Thinking and Organizational Learning Program, Senge offers the reader an opportunity to rise above conventional ideas, all the while staying in touch with concrete organizations and their experiences.

CHAPTER SIX

Society Run Amok

People of every political and philosophical persuasion seem agreed that modern organizations have a number of problems. Often their complaints focus on bureaucracy, but the unhappiness is broader than that. In this chapter, we examine some of the factors that lead social structure to "go bad."

There is no shortage of critics of modern society. They are found among academic scholars, in the popular press, and in the conversations of everyday life. You probably can count yourself among the critics, as can I. In too many ways, the systems we've constructed just don't seem to work—or at least they don't work as well as we think they could or should.

Some complaints are directed at particular power groups in society: big corporations or big labor unions, the Democratic or Republican Party, the military-industrial complex, organized religion, or "cultural elites." Some blame capitalism or socialism, as systems that implement particular philosophies and have certain consequences. Sometimes "bureaucracy" is blamed regardless of the social or political philosophies it may be intended to support. Some people simply blame "the system."

In this chapter, I take a somewhat different approach to the problems we experience with social structure. Rather than look for the source of social problems in the misdeeds of specific individuals or groups or in the philosophies of particular systems, I look more deeply into the nature of systems per se and into the interactions between individuals and systems.

THE PROBLEM WITH SYSTEMS

Instead of blaming "the system," French sociologist Jacques Ellul suggested that something more fundamental was the source of our problems. In his *The Technological Society* (1954/1964), Ellul said the problem was imbedded in the very idea of *technique.* Given the many ways of doing almost anything, Ellul found humans inclined to search for the "one best way" of doing anything and everything. "Technical activity is the most primitive activity of man. There is the technique of hunting, of fishing, of food gathering; and later of weapons, clothing, and building. . . . Magic developed along with other techniques as an expression of man's will to obtain certain results of a spiritual order" (pp. 23-34).

Although the development of techniques has been with us from the beginning, it reached new heights with the Industrial Revolution: "This systematization, unification, and clarification was applied to everything—it resulted not only in the establishment of budgetary rules and in fiscal organization, but in the systematization of weights and measures and the planning of roads" (Ellul, 1954/1964, p. 43).

Every time we settle on a technique for doing things, we surrender the freedom to do them in other ways. Technique is, therefore, inherently opposed to freedom.

Reminiscent of our earlier discussions of autopoiesis, Ellul found that the technical order had become *self-augmenting:* "Technique has arrived at such a point in its evolution that it is being transformed and is progressing almost without decisive intervention by man" (p. 85).

The end result of the systematization of human affairs is too often a nightmare of impersonal and dehumanized relations. Hear how cancer patient Bob Secter (1992) described his experience of organized medicine.

> What I experienced, what all too many other patients have experienced as well, was truly a Doctor Hell. It's a twilight zone of bureaucracy, nearsightedness and detachment that can defeat or at least complicate even the best efforts of the most sincere and dedicated medical professionals, of whom there are many. . . . (p. 16)
>
> Doctor Hell, where what's best for the patient sometimes takes a back seat to what's best for the institution and its bureaucracy, will live on regardless of whether those it cares for do. (p. 37)

MAYBE THE SYSTEMS WORK JUST FINE

As the preceding comments confirm, there is no shortage of criticism about the failure of social structure to deliver on its promise to human beings. For a moment, however, it will be useful for us to consider a radically different point of view, one that perhaps will empower us to address the perceived problem more effectively.

Put most bluntly, I suggest that (a) social structure works just fine—in doing what it's designed to do—and (b) any perceived failures are the fault of the humans rather than of the systems. Seen from a slightly different angle, let's consider the possibility that our organizations would work just fine except that they make assumptions about our behavior that *we* don't deliver on. Whereas the humanists complain that our modern institutions don't measure up to what it really means to be human, it will be useful to consider the possibility that we don't live up to the potential that is contained within our social structures. I'm not arguing that we are ultimately at fault, but I think you'll find value in exploring that possibility.

To kick off the conversation, it might be useful to talk about "the failure of communism." After decades of a cold war that divided Americans into those who were reluctant to criticize communism and those who enjoyed nothing better, there is now agreement that communism failed. The ideological commitments maintained among the political left have suffered a death blow from observations of the economic, political, and environmental disasters that occured among the Soviet bloc nations.

In the face of such general agreement, I suggest the possibility that communism failed because we humans were inferior to the challenge. Nothing was wrong with communism except that the human beings who tried it out weren't good enough to make it work. In fact, let's consider the possibility that 100 years from now or 1,000 years from now, people will look back on the Marxist experiment of the 20th century and say that human beings simply hadn't evolved sufficiently to make it work.

I know these comments may seem so outrageous to you as to preclude serious attention, but a part of the excitement of sociology comes in the ability—indeed the requirement—to explore ideas that do not immediately seem all that smart. In this particular instance, I draw your attention to the fact that communism is the oldest and most successful form of social organization that humans have tried.

The family is the best example of communism you will find. This point is seen most clearly in the Marxist (1875) dictum: "From each according to his abilities, to each according to his needs" (Tucker, p. 388). What is contributed is held in common by the collective, and the needs of individual members are drawn from that common pool. This technique is exactly how successful families operate. Each member is expected to contribute what he or she is capable of contributing to the collective unit, and each has a claim on whatever he or she needs—regardless of the contributions.

Notice how implicitly the communist principle denies the principle of equality. The members of a family are definitely not expected to contribute equally: Adults are expected to contribute more than young children, and young adults in an extended family are expected to contribute more than their elderly parents. These expectations cannot be stated in terms of specific ages; the bottom line is that everyone contributes according to his or her ability.

There is no equality in what individuals get out of a family, either: They receive according to their needs. Inevitably some get more than others, though the principles defining their needs can vary. Sometimes the needs of dependent children always come first, whereas other patterns favor the adult hunter-warriors or pregnant women. Never are the members of a family expected to take strictly equal shares of what's held in common by the family. Imagine how you would have felt if your parents had denied you a needed operation on the basis of your having already used up your medical allotment.

This scenario was the basis for a comic rejoinder in the successful *Cosby Show*. When Cosby's character, Cliff Huxtable, vetoed a family expenditure proposed by the family's children, one of them complained, "Why can't we do it? We're rich." Cosby, who portrayed a successful obstetrician (and who doesn't do that badly in real life), replied, "No, your mother and I are rich; you are poor." The humor in his retort underscores my fundamental belief that the family is a communist organization.

This episode also points out that *power* is not shared equally within the family. In matriarchal families, the wife-mother wields the greater power; in patriarchal families, the husband-father is in control. Even in societies with an egalitarian norm for husbands and wives, it is a rare family in which it is not possible to identify one or the other partner as having a greater say in what the collective does. And in no family do small children share equally with their parents in power. Notice, in fact, that when parents may consciously grant their children more of a say as they mature, it is the parents who are giving a share of the power to their children.

So the family is a communist organization, and it has been remarkably successful. The fundamental principles of communism work admirably, and families fail when individuals' commitments to those principles weaken. Liberals and conservatives alike look down on the able-bodied adult who refuses to provide for the needs of his or her family. Children who fail to abide by parental authority and refuse their "share" of chores are seen as dysfunctional members of the family. If the family fails to function properly, we never criticize the idea or the ideal of the family; rather, we look for failures among its members.

It is worth noting that communism has sometimes been successful on a larger scale than families. In small religious communities and in some of Israel's communal *kibbutzim*, unrelated individuals have been able to come together and consciously bind themselves together in accordance with communist principles. Interestingly they often refer to themselves as a family, highlighting the links between communism and family by their use of that metaphor.

So why has communism failed so badly on a larger scale? Although scholars can offer complex explanations for the failure, a simpler one will serve our present purposes. Communism failed in Eastern Europe because the individuals involved weren't up to it. They weren't willing to abide by the fundamental principles. Factory managers who misappropriated state resources for their own use violated the principles; so did the workers who stayed home from work or malingered on the job.

Try to imagine what the U.S.S.R. would have been like if everyone had contributed actively to the state whatever he or she was capable of and if everyone respected the needs of others in making his or her own demands on the system. The U.S. would be asking the U.S.S.R. for loans, rather than the reverse. Instead people established a social organization grounded in a certain set of principles, and then they behaved in terms of other principles.

There's an old Vermont joke about the farmer with his first tractor, crashing headlong into a stone wall, shouting "Whoa!" The tractor was true to its design principles, but the hapless farmer was operating according to a different set of principles. The same was true of the Marxist experiment in Europe.

So if communism failed in Europe because the participants were marching to a different drummer, can we identify the principle(s) they were committed to? At the risk of oversimplifying, I think it would be accurate to identify *individualism* as the primary principle that conflicted with communism in the European experiment. Communism, which assumes that individuals will sacrifice their own personal and individual interests to those of the collective, is in direct opposition to the value of individualism, which has had strong support in European cultures and is fundamental to American culture.

When Americans speak of "human dignity" and "the sanctity of human life," they are paying homage to the value of individualism. It was the American commitment to this value that accounted for the ferocity with which many Americans resisted the idea of communism throughout the cold war. Even if Marx's dialectical materialism had not given his version of communism an atheistic dimension, many Americans would have seen it as "godless" anyway. Communism posed the most fundamental kind of threat to what Americans traditionally have held most sacred: the position that any person, no matter how lowly his or her origins, possesses the ability to rise to any heights.

Seymour Martin Lipset (1963), the political sociologist, suggested that American political history can be seen as an ongoing struggle between two fundamental values: achievement and equality. The struggle derives from the inherent incompatibility between these two values that we hold dear. After all, the freedom for individuals to achieve anything that lies within the grasp of their abilities means, on the one hand, the freedom to surpass others: to be *unequal.* The commitment to equality, on the other hand, is an inherent damper on individual achievement.

In gross comparison, liberals and the Democratic Party in the U.S. have addressed this conflict with a bias toward equality, whereas the bias of conservatives and the Republican Party has been toward achievement. Thus the Democrats have been more consistent in their support for social programs such as Social Security, minimum wage, unemployment insurance, welfare, and progressive taxation, while the Republicans have been more committed to using unfettered capitalism as a vehicle for individuals to amass whatever wealth they were capable of, resisting government regulation of business, for example, and favoring tax breaks on capital gains. Ironically these orientations put liberals in the position of favoring government restraints on individual freedom, whereas liberalism initially arose in opposition to government suppression of individual liberty. (Often our concepts are more consistent than the language we use to represent them.)

During the cold war hysteria, conservatives sometimes accused liberals of being communists or communist sympathizers. This accusation is valid only to the extent that communism requires restraints on individualism on behalf of the collective good. It is fair to say, however, that American liberals would not put nearly enough limits on individualism to make communism work.

Communism might stand a better chance of success in Asia than in Europe, because there is generally less commitment to individualism in most Asian cultures. This deemphasis was brought home to me during travels in Asia during 1991.

I was in Malaysia, for example, at the time a United Nations report rated the nations of the world on the basis of (a) economic development and (b) human rights. Malaysia was ranked relatively high on the first, low on the second. At the time, the Malaysian government was pursuing a program called Twenty Twenty Vision, which represented its commitment to be listed among the developed nations of the world by the year 2020. Thus the UN's acknowledgement of the progress in that regard was welcomed. However, criticism of Malaysia's record on human rights was addressed with great official scorn. On May 25, 1991, Malaysia's *New Straits Times* carried a front page article entitled "Dr. M: Freedom Has Its Limits."

> Anyone claiming that Malaysia lacked human freedom should also look at the records of some developed countries where varied levels of discrimination are obvious, Datuk Seri Dr. Mahathir Mohammad said today.
>
> The Prime Minister said Malaysia did not want to have human freedom to the extent that the people could riot in the streets and burn houses to give vent to their feelings.
>
> "If this is what is meant by freedom then I do not want it," Dr. Mahathir said at a Press conference at the end of his four-day visit to Sarawak. ("Dr. M: Freedom," 1991, p. 1)

In the days that followed, the prime minister elaborated his views on the nature of individual freedom and democracy in Asia. The May 26th front page headline declared "We Won't Compromise."

> He said Malaysia preferred not to be grouped with such countries labelled as having high levels of human freedom but which condone nudity and allow pornographic materials to be made freely available.
>
> The Prime Minister said there were reports of a European country, categorized as having a very high level of human freedom, where free sex was practiced and where even 12-year-olds were known to be allowed to have sexual relationships.
>
> "If this is what is meant by a high level of human freedom, we do not want it," he told reporters after chairing a three hour Umno supreme council meeting at the party's headquarters. ("We Won't," 1991, p. 1)

By May 27th, Dr. Mahathir was warning of "agents of Western countries."

> He said the Western style of democracy of placing individual freedom above the community was not suitable for Malaysia.

Earlier, in his speech to the community leaders, he cited cases where individuals in the West could act in the name of personal freedom and jeopardize the community's morals.

He said a decent small-town community in the United States could not stop an X-rated cinema from operating within their midst even though the entire community did not want it there.

He added that if personal freedom was given too much emphasis, what was at one time frowned upon would eventually be acceptable because everyone was allowed to "do his own thing."

He cited instances of marriages and divorces between homosexuals and between lesbians as examples. ("Dr. M Warns," 1991, p. 2)

Rather than deny any of the specific charges regarding the suppression of individual freedom, then, the government criticized the standards being applied in that regard. It was suggested that the countries most reflecting the UN's standards for human rights were also societies besieged with problems of crime, drug abuse, prostitution, and the like. Thus the Malaysian government took some pride in controlling what it saw as the excesses of unfettered individualism. Quite specifically, it argued that the individualistic extremism of the West couldn't work in Asia, with its traditionally greater commitment to the family and the state.

There is a powerful irony here. Malaysian society in 1991 was strongly anticommunist. Nonetheless the official view of the balance between individual liberty and the common good was tipped in the direction required for communism to work.

At about the same time the Malaysian government was discussing the UN report on human rights, the *Straits Times* of Singapore was examining the question of whether this tiny island nation at the tip of the Malay Peninsula was overregulated. The preponderance of fines for numerous offenses had led to a popular joke about Singapore being a "fine" city. Associate Editor Bob Ng (1991) posed the question: Do Singaporeans deserve the rules they get? After interviews with readers, he concluded the following:

Before attempting an answer, let's consider the backdrop against which we interact with one another. Small island. Lots of people. Most in HDB flats [government housing]. Neighbourhoods close together. Many cars. Not enough roads. Schools, shopping plazas, entertainment spots, leisure places, food centres, markets—most of the time teeming with people.

In this context, without rules, our daily social intercourse with one another would be full of friction. Here rules help to lubricate relations between fellow citizens, smoothening what otherwise would be abrasive points.

The Prime Minister put it this way in his end-April speech: "To create social space, we need rules. The ideal is to let customs and social etiquette determine our social space. But since we have not yet arrived at the ideal state, we will need rules to regulate our behaviour." (p. 26)

Just 2 years before these discussions, of course, in the People's Republic of China, Premier Li Peng had sent tanks and soldiers to fire on students gathered in Tiananmen Square, saying their demands for individual freedom amounted to anarchy. It seems a safe generalization that the nations of Asia—whether identified as communist or anticommunist—have cultural traditions that place far less importance on individual rights than is taken for granted in Europe and the United States.

Notice also that these comments are reminiscent of discussions of Japanese business practices. In contrast to American patterns, Japanese workers are much more likely to feel personal loyalty to the company and responsibility for its success.

These lengthy comments about individualism and communism are directly relevant to our more general analysis of how social structure works—and particularly how it fails to work. The establishment of any organization involves the establishment of a collective entity that has its own survival needs, and the survival of the organization is held to be in the interest of the individuals who participate in it. Although most capitalist business firms surely would object to being called communist, there is a sense in which that is an accurate description. Surely the most successful companies would be those in which all individuals contributed to the fullest extent of their abilities and each received what he or she needed to be effective.

In less inflammatory language, we are safe in saying that all organizations are based on the assumption that individuals will be willing, to some extent, to set aside their individual interests in favor of the collective interests of the organization. That's all the company store asks of each of us. Let's see how well we deliver on the assumption.

THE PLACE OF RESPONSIBILITY

Recall earlier discussions in which we concluded that social structure was made of surrendered individual freedom and that it was organized through agreements. If human beings were incapable of breaking their promises, that would be the end of the story. We would all agree to do our parts in the corporate enterprise, we would do what we said, and everything would work out as expected.

Now take a moment to review your own behavior and what you've observed of others—and see whether you think this would be a reasonable way to proceed. To what extent are you willing to trust others to voluntarily set their self-interest aside in favor of the common good? Chances are you'd be wary about counting on that.

Regardless of your own beliefs and experiences in this regard, it is clear that we do not base our social structure on the faith that people simply will do what's right. Earlier we looked at the concepts of *norms* and *sanctions* in tandem: What you're expected to do is coupled with what will happen to you if you don't do it. You're expected to drive under 25 miles an hour on Elm Street, and you'll pay a fine if you're caught violating that expectation. We have agreed not to steal other people's stuff, and we'll go to prison if we're caught doing so.

Notice that the mere existence of sanctions shifts responsibility for keeping our agreements from us to the system. Before exploring that process further, however, let's acknowledge that it is only part of the story. Sometimes we take our agreements so much to heart that we police our own compliance. The social scientific term *internalization* refers to this possibility.

I'm willing to bet that your failure to kill people who annoy you is based on something more than the fear that you might be caught and punished. Chances are you just wouldn't feel right about it. Maybe you have religious beliefs that add a new dimension to the possibility of punishment, but, even lacking that, most of us have so internalized the view that murder is wrong that we just couldn't do it. You may feel that way about stealing; even if there was no way anyone would ever find out, you'd know you did it and you'd feel bad.

Imagine that you are driving through the outskirts of a small town at 3:00 in the morning. No other car is in sight, and you haven't even seen one for half an hour. You come to a stop light at a deserted intersection. You can see half a mile in every direction, and no other cars are on the road. Furthermore there is no place for the police to be hiding at this intersection. The traffic light turns red just as you arrive. Do you (a) drive through the light, (b) stop, look, and drive through, or (c) sit and wait for the light to change?

If you chose (c) above, you've had another direct encounter with internalization. If you just "wouldn't feel right" going through the red light, that feeling is precisely what would make social structure work flawlessly all the time. If you feel bad about the realization that you might sit at the deserted intersection, waiting for some electric light to give you permission to go along your way, you're experiencing the fundamental dilemma we face in living together.

All of us internalize the agreements of society to some extent, and none of us do it completely. In any event, however, we design our social structure on the assumption that internalization is not enough to ensure that the humans will keep their agreements. Thus we establish sanctions, and, in so doing, we shift responsibility from individuals to society. We establish what sociologists call *agents of social control:* parents, teachers, police, and others.

Once we've assigned responsibility for enforcement to someone else, it seems inevitable that we ease up on our own responsibility to some extent. We create the possibility of getting away with breaking the agreements, which is very difficult when you are the one nagging you to comply.

When responsibility for enforcement of the agreements shifts from individuals to the agents of the whole, often an increase in deviance occurs: the breaking of agreements. If I believe there is nothing particularly sacred about an agreement (I haven't internalized it) and I'm pretty sure I won't get caught violating it, I'm that much more likely to do so: I remove the label from the pillow and throw it away in a public trash can far from my home. I cross a deserted street in the face of DON'T WALK. I strike a match without closing the cover and believe I've struck a blow for human dignity in the process.

Whenever we transfer the responsibility for keeping us in line to someone else, we enhance the possibility of resentment, resistance, and revolt. The resulting increase in deviance has its own consequence. What do we do when the sanctions don't seem to be working, when individuals aren't keeping their agreements? Typically we add new sanctions, make them more punitive, and/or increase the number of agents of social control.

If chewing gum in high school will get the chewer an hour of detention after school and students are chewing gum anyway, the "logical" solution is to increase the penalty to 5 hours of detention and perhaps to institute random mouth inspections. This beefing up of social control, however, is likely to result in an increase in last-minute gum swallowing. That ploy could be countered, however, by offering students a day's excused absence for informing on gum chewers and testifying against them at Gum Court. This fundamental dialectic of deviance and deterrence is being enacted all around you every day.

Consider the matter of taxes. Certain inevitable costs are involved in having an organized society, and it would seem reasonable for all of us to chip in. Thus we institute a system of taxation, specifying how much each of us should pay. Because we don't assume that everyone will pay his or her fair share, we establish mechanisms for enforcement: the Internal Revenue Service, for example. Of course, having an IRS is an added expense, thereby raising the amount of the taxes we must pay.

Perhaps in our resentment over having to pay the salaries of the enforcers, some of us look around for loopholes to reduce how much we have to pay. Some of us may simply cheat. As a result, not enough taxes are collected, and it is necessary to raise the overall tax rates to compensate for the shortfall, to make the tax laws more complicated in order to close the loopholes, and to increase the number of enforcement agents to catch the cheaters. All of these actions increase the cost of collecting taxes and, hence, the amount each of us is expected to pay. That increase increases the incentive to find ways of avoiding taxes, which generates more efforts to counter the avoidance—which always comes at an increased cost.

The growing desire to avoid excessive taxes results in the appearance of professional tax consultants. Because these people only consult for a fee, it is necessary for us to find ways of saving enough on our taxes to make it all worthwhile. And the consultants have to earn enough to be able to pay their own taxes. If the tax consultants do their jobs too well, of course, that produces another tax shortfall, producing more complicated tax laws, making the use of tax consultants all the more essential (and more expensive, because their job has become harder and requires more preparatory schooling). Moreover, it has become necessary to enact laws to regulate the behavior of tax consultants—and the employment, training, and supervision of agents to keep the tax consultants in line.

As if all of this weren't bad enough, another dimension makes matters even worse. Whenever we discover (or even have a feeling) that people are breaking the agreements, we have a tendency to rewrite the rules rather than simply to search out the alleged offenders and make them stop. Here's an example.

Every university harbors the belief that some of the faculty are not living up to their teaching responsibilities. For example, deans and chairs whisper about how *some faculty* are coming to class late and/or are leaving early on a regular basis. Others are rumored to be bad teachers, not knowing and/or caring about how to educate students. Specifically it may be alleged that some faculty refuse to prepare any course materials, such as syllabi, reading lists, and so forth—documents that would give some order to the course and make it more useful to students.

Anyone committed to education probably would agree that such behavior is inappropriate for faculty and that something should be done, though protecting the norm of academic freedom. The logical action, perhaps, would be to identify the guilty parties and to talk with them. The offending faculty members' chairs or deans might discuss the problem and offer assistance in the design and preparation of appropriate course materials. If the faculty members in question were untenured, such "suggestions" would carry more weight than if they had tenure, but even in the latter case, peer pressure would very likely produce the desired change in behavior.

In practice, a very different approach is more likely to be taken. Rather than identify the offending faculty (asking a few students would accomplish this), administrators are more likely to devise additional rules and procedures that, while applying to all faculty, should avoid the problems rumored to exist in the case of a few. At Chapman University, for example, *all* faculty are required to prepare course syllabi and submit them to the dean for review. This procedure may not seem like a big imposition, but notice that it adds an additional burden on faculty who presumably were doing nothing wrong; more important, it sends a message that they are not trusted to teach their courses properly.

Slightly bruised feelings aside, what is the likely result of this new procedure in the case of faculty who presumably were at fault? They are the most likely to ignore the requirement of submitting syllabi to the dean. Sometimes matters end here. The faculty who were already preparing course materials will have been irritated and slightly inconvenienced, and those at fault would not have improved. Typically this unhappy situation calls for Phase Two from the administrators' handbook.

More memos are circulated, insisting on the importance of submitting syllabi to the dean for review. Department chairs are charged with the responsibility for collecting syllabi and reviewing them before forwarding them to the dean. Firm deadlines are established for stages one and two of the revised procedure. Now all faculty have been further offended, the chairs have been given additional duties (when they really had enough to do), and the offending faculty are the most likely to ignore the new procedure just as they did the initial one.

In the interest of brevity, let's assume that the offending faculty are finally badgered into preparing and filing syllabi. Given their demonstrated resistance to preparing such materials, along with their inexperience in doing so, chances are good that the syllabi finally submitted by such faculty will be poor in quality. They will not really solve the problem that initially spurred the chain of administrative requirements.

Rather than review the inadequate syllabi with the offending faculty, it is more likely that the administration will issue detailed instructions on the length of and format for syllabi. As before, the regulation will apply to all faculty. Those who have been preparing thoughtful syllabi for decades are likely to find the formats they have been using do not measure up to the administratively established standard. Some of these faculty will put in the necessary effort to revise their syllabi, doing so with great resentment and frustration. Others will ignore the standardized format, choosing to stay with the materials they think have been successful with students. These latter faculty may find themselves in protracted discussions with the dean over their failure to conform to the standard. The offending faculty probably will be spared such discussions because they will have neglected to submit anything.

This scenario is enacted in organizations around the world countless times each day. If it is suspected that some employees are misappropriating company supplies, the most common solution is to increase the paperwork required for requisitioning all supplies, and perhaps accounting for inventory will be made more complex as well. The result is that employees who had done nothing wrong must now spend time on paperwork designed to thwart the presumed offenses of others. Morale goes down as the "good" employees are told they are not trusted. Those who had been misappropriating supplies—if there really were any in the first place—simply find ways around the new regulations. When it becomes apparent that the new regulations haven't solved anything, it is likely that even more complex procedures will be established, making matters worse. In fact, it soon will be necessary to hire new administrative staff to monitor the increased paperwork, to complain when employees do not follow the procedures, and to withhold supplies that might be essential to getting the official job done. Morale decreases further, and the "good" employees must start cheating on the regulations in order to get their jobs done.

Earlier, when we talked about the invention of bureaucracy, we saw that bureaucracy represented an advance over the inconsistency, disorganization, and whimsy that characterized earlier forms of administration. Great advantage can be gained from the establishment of standard procedures—sometimes. Two problems undercut this advantage. First, sometimes unusual situations require ad hoc responses.

Bureaucracies and bureaucrats are most often ridiculed for the mindless application of procedures that are clearly inappropriate to the situation at hand. The converse of this problem, as we've seen above, is the design of generalized procedures that are really appropriate only in a few unusual cases.

Second, the advantage of generalized procedures is weakened by the process of *reification*. To *reify* is to believe something is real when it is not. In the present case, this problem shows up when we attribute moral significance to procedures that are really just something we made up. For example, the standardized syllabus format discussed above might actually be well thought out and generally a useful model to follow. It becomes reified when people treat it as the Word of God and treat failure to comply as a mortal sin. Reification has occurred whenever a particular requirement is ultimately justified as "That's the rule!"

Reification typically is required in the process of internalization, discussed above. There you are, sitting at a red light, following the natural catastrophe that has left you the sole surviving human on Planet Earth. If you wait for the light to turn green, because it just wouldn't feel right to do otherwise, you have reified the rule. There is nothing wrong with the rule, by the way. In fact, it is extremely useful for letting us all drive on the same highways with a minimum of carnage. Still it is only a rule of convenience; it is not a law of nature.

To review, we have seen how the establishment of social structure typically involves a shift of responsibility from individuals to the group. More accurately, the creation of organized social relations involves a shift of responsibility from rank-and-file individuals to those few individuals officially responsible for the group as a whole: the CEO, for example. And the way administrative responsibility is exercised can have the effect of further reducing the sense of responsibility felt and acted on among the rank and file.

FREEDOM AND ADMINISTRATIVE LEADERSHIP

Earlier I spoke of freedom as a possibility or an option. Freedom, in this sense, is the key to understanding important differences in leadership styles. The conventional model of leadership is to take away people's options. Traditionally power has been seen as the ability to make others do what you want them to do. In the Marine Corps, I was taught that inspired leadership was making people want to do the things they had to do. In either case, we are talking about limiting people's possibilities or options.

A fundamentally different kind of leadership is that which increases people's options. This is what is meant by supporting those working for you; it is seen in the leaders who define their jobs as learning what their workers need in order to do their jobs and providing it. The term *empowerment* often is used in this respect.

Taylorism, discussed in Chapter 3, offers a clear example of the first kind of leadership: Structure the work so that individuals have the minimum number of choices to make. As we saw, the ideal was to get individuals to behave as much like machine parts as possible.

As an aside, the lack of freedom is what produces alienation in individuals. Ironically Marx understood this, but Marxism—seeking to constrain political freedom—ended up limiting choices in the workplace more than capitalism. Everything Marx warned against in this respect came true more patently in socialist than in capitalist societies. It is worth noting that the socialist societies were quite taken by Taylor's (1911) idea of scientific management.

These two leadership styles also make opposite assumptions about human nature. The first assumes that people will do the wrong thing unless you force them to do what they should; the second assumes that people want to do what's right and sometimes are prevented from doing so. Empowerment means removing the obstacles that lie in the way of people doing what's right.

You may know someone who fits the model of an empowering leader: someone who seemed to trust you to do the right thing and who seemed focused on removing the obstacles to your doing just that. On the other hand, I'm sure you know the other type of leader: one who seemed to believe the worst about you and sought as much control over you as possible. The latter kind seem more common. You might reflect back on your parents and teachers as leaders in these regards.

Some administrators have a personality need to control others and seek organizational positions that satisfy that need. That's not the whole story, however. Administrators have an *official* responsibility for the success, well-being, and survival of organizations. In a university, for example, an individual faculty member will feel responsible for providing classroom instruction, evaluating students, advising, and similar tasks. Each of these faculty functions is important to the success and survival of the university as a whole, and yet a faculty member could do his or her job perfectly and the university could still perish. Perhaps other faculty were less diligent. Or perhaps the Vice President for

Finance miscalculated the tuition needed to cover expenses. Or perhaps the admissions staff failed to enroll enough incoming students to keep the university afloat.

Although an individual faculty member would have a definite interest in the other sources of organizational failure and would have a personal stake in the matter, it is the administrator who is responsible for making all of the parts of the whole come together for organizational survival.

Unfortunately this situation tends to separate faculty and administrators in modern universities as solidly as the social classes of Marx's analyses. This imagery is exacerbated by the fact that administrators earn much more money than faculty, have better offices and equipment, and are supported by larger staffs. The structuring of responsibility in this fashion can produce dysfunctional behavior on the part of the finest humans. Charged with responsibility for organizational survival, administrators have an understandable tendency to seek control over the elements that affect survival, particularly the budget. A concomitant attempt is made to exclude faculty (and others) from decision making.

Charging administrators with responsibility for organizational survival has the effect of letting faculty off the hook in that regard. Excluding them from decision making further enforces that view. Thus faculty are likely to focus their attention of personal self-interest on the interests of their local portions of the university (e.g., their departments).

To the extent that faculty work for personal or local interests within the university, that is likely to create problems for the survival of the whole. Such problems create a greater challenge for the administrators and encourage them to become more and more controlling. The result is a cycle of growing conflict and despair.

As in the case of The Holiday Project (see Chapter 1), I have had the opportunity to see this situation from different vantage points: in this case, as a professor and as a college vice-president. I have had an opportunity to see the intrauniversity class struggle from both sides of the barricades. My biggest disappointment as a full-time administrator was the feeling that I no longer was involved in higher education.

To some extent, managing colleges and universities has become more and more similar to managing insurance companies or department stores. The respected philosopher of education, Jacques Barzun (1991), recently was prompted to observe:

> Today, a labor negotiator would make a better president than a philosopher such as Nicholas Murray Butler or a chemist such as Charles W.

Eliot. The future university man may have to draw on retired Mafia chiefs. . . .

The work of higher education presupposes some agreement about two things: the contents of the tradition being handed down and extended by research and the limits of the portion suitable and required for undergraduate instruction—the curriculum. At this moment, no such agreement exists. (p. B1)

COMMUNITARIANISM

The dilemma we've been examining with regard to individual freedom and the needs of the group is a fundamental one. One sociologist who has become particularly concerned about it is Amatai Etzioni, a specialist in the study of organizations.

In 1991, Etzioni began publishing a journal entitled *The Responsive Community*, aimed at promoting what he had labeled *communitarianism*. The main thrust of Etzioni's effort was to find a way of establishing a balance between rights and responsibilities in a modern democracy. The "Responsive Communitarian Platform" (Etzioni, 1991/2) states, in part:

A communitarian perspective recognizes that the preservation of individual liberty depends on the active maintenance of the institutions of civil society where citizens learn respect for others as well as self-respect; where we acquire a lively sense of our personal and civic responsibilities, along with an appreciation of our own rights and the rights of others; where we develop the skills of self-government as well as the habit of governing ourselves, and learn to serve others—not just self. (p. 4)

The basic communitarian quest for balances between individuals and groups, rights and responsibilities, and among the institutions of state, market, and civil society is a constant, ongoing enterprise. Because this quest takes place within history and within varying social contexts, however, the evaluation of what is a proper moral stance will vary according to circumstances of time and place. If we were in China today, we would argue vigorously for more individual rights; in contemporary America, we emphasize individual and social responsibilities. (pp. 5-6)

It is much too early to know what impact Etzioni will have within the sociological profession and among the general public, but the issue he has identified is precisely the one we've seen that lies so often at the root of failure for social structure.

CONCLUSION

The failure of social structure has proven a more complex phenomenon than it might have first seemed. Whereas people often complain about aspects of social structure (such as bureaucracy), we've seen more clearly in this chapter that social structure not only is our creation but also survives only through our participation in it. *How* it works depends on how we work it.

A key element in the operation of social structure is how we see and act on our responsibility in the matter. Because social structure is created out of surrendered freedom, there is a natural tendency for us to relinquish responsibility in the bargain. If I'm giving up my freedom in agreeing to do what you (as leader) say, it makes sense to hold you responsible for how it all turns out.

Unfortunately, when individuals give up some of their freedom and also give up responsibility for the collective outcome, they often tend to continue looking out for their own interests. And when the needs of the collective effort conflict with their own needs, they opt for the latter if they think they can get away with it.

To make matters worse, as we have seen, the leaders who take on responsibility for the collective effort do not necessarily give up concerns for their own self-interests. Again, when the two conflict, the leaders often may look out for themselves rather than for the interests of the whole. Hence the newspapers are filled with stories of corruption and malfeasance at the highest levels in society.

Thus we have seen that the problems we experience are not necessarily the "fault" of the social structures we've created, but rather lie in how we interact with those social structures. However, it is possible to establish social structures that, in their very design, produce results we may agree are evil. The next chapter is devoted to the identification of such cases of defective social structure.

Points of Discussion

- Recall a run-in you've had with some form of social structure recently. What was the role of other humans in the conflict?

- Give some examples of ways you've relinquished responsibility for collective success when you join together with others to accomplish something.

■ Give examples of the two types of leaders described in the chapter: emphasizing control, or support of those under them.

Reading Further

Several popular books elaborate on the foibles of social structure; I've referred to some in the text of this chapter. Chronologically the first I'll mention here is C. Northcote Parkinson's classic *Parkinson's Law* (Boston: Houghton Mifflin, 1957). Parkinson's central observation was that the time it would take to complete a piece of work was determined by the amount of time allowed for its completion. Ask for a report in 4 weeks, and it will take 4 weeks for the report to be written.

Laurence J. Peter and Raymond Hull's work *The Peter Principle* (New York: Bantam, 1969) notes an unintended design flaw in most organizations: Although it makes sense to promote people when they perform well at an assigned job but makes no sense to promote them when they perform badly, people rise in the organization hierarchy until they reach a job they are unqualified for—and that's where they stay. The result, in the phrase used by the authors, is that everyone will rise to his or her "level of incompetence."

In a more recent entry, John Gall offers *Systemantics: How Systems Really Work and How They Fail* (Ann Arbor, MI: General Systemantics, 1988), in which he catalogs numerous design flaws in systems. Gall's central thesis, which he calls the Primal Scenario, is: "Systems in general work poorly or not at all" (p. 6). That quote should give you some idea of the tenor of the book. Gall is particularly interested in how the systems we create to solve problems usually end up creating problems of their own. This result is especially true of complex systems, which tend to generate unpredictable results. Here's an example to illustrate Gall's point: "The largest building in the world, the Space Vehicle Preparation Shed at Cape Canaveral, *generates its own weather, including clouds and rain.* Designed to protect space rockets from the elements, it pelts them with storms of its own" (Gall, 1988, p. 24).

CHAPTER SEVEN

Sociological Diagnostics

In this chapter, we apply the principles discussed previously to a set of social problems, showing how the sociological perspective can provide a special approach to the identification of and solution to a wide range of social problems.

A key purpose of this book has been to show that social structure exists in a domain that cannot be reduced to individual psychology. By the same token, social problems cannot be dealt with on the level of the individual alone. This recognition led the sociologist C. Wright Mills (1959) to distinguish between personal troubles and social problems. Thus, when a particular person loses his or her job, that is a *personal trouble* for that person and for those who may be dependent on him or her; but when unemployment in a society's economy is high, that is a *social problem.* In this chapter, I suggest some approaches to the diagnosis and treatment of social problems—at the level of social structure.

Just as physicians deal with the health problems of human patients, sociological practitioners deal with the health problems of social structure, such as organizations, institutions, and whole societies. As with physicians, three steps are involved in dealing with the health problems of social structure.

First, it is necessary to make observations relevant to diagnosing the situation. Thus the physician takes your temperature and looks down your throat. In this context, I want to introduce the notion of *sociological diagnostics* as an application of social indicators research. For example, I will deal with the current concern over affirmative action and the red herring of "quotas." We'll see how the logic of multivariate analysis makes it easily possible to distinguish legitimate criteria from prejudice in analyzing the status of women or ethnic minorities.

Second, the physician makes a diagnosis: You have a cold, for example. The sociologist might conclude, for example, that the banks in a community are discriminating against blacks or single women.

Third, the physician prescribes a treatment: rest, drink lots of liquids, and take two aspirins every 4 hours, for example. The sociologist might work with the banks with an eye to sensitizing their employees to the problem, or it might be appropriate to draft legislation, to work with consumer groups in bringing suit in court, or to implement other remedies.

Despite the parallels between the sick individual and the sick society, there is one vital difference the sociologist needs to keep in mind. The human body basically is designed to repair itself (which is the main theme in the case of "curing" the common cold), and even when the physician engages in fairly radical procedures, the body is always the physician's ally in the cure. If the body does repair itself, we call that a success, and the human being occupying the body is happy about the outcome.

In the case of society, as we've seen repeatedly, the autopoietic quality of social structure means that it also is designed to remedy its own problems, and indeed the sociologist must work in concert with that capacity for self-repair. However, social structure will not necessarily repair itself in ways that we deem successful. It is worth noting that the human body often heals itself by sacrificing some of its parts. Millions of cells may be burned up in the process of destroying a cold, for example, but we don't worry about those cells. In the case of social structure, however, we are the cells.

In the Nazis' pursuit of Aryan supremacy in World War II, millions of human beings were burned in the ovens of Buchenwald, Dachau, and Auschwitz. Similarly social structure may heal economic imbalances by making millions unemployed and homeless. The perpetuation of religious values and beliefs may be achieved at the expense of broken bodies in the torture chambers of an inquisition or the millions of young people bleeding and dead on the battlefields of holy wars. Although social structure is designed to heal itself, it is often at the expense of the humans living there. One task of the sociologist is to find cures that support the individuals, as well as the organizing process that is social structure.

In the remainder of this chapter, most of our attention is addressed to sociological diagnosis, with less attention to cures. First, I locate this activity within the field of sociology in general. Next, we look at the logic of multivariate analysis. Then we consider some concrete examples of how that logic might be applied.

SOCIOLOGICAL PRACTICE

The subject of this chapter falls primarily in half of a dichotomy scientists sometimes make: between pure and applied research. *Applied sociology* involves the application of sociological theories, discoveries, and techniques to specific issues in social life. Whereas most "pure" sociology is carried on within universities, applied sociology is practiced both within and outside academic settings. Outside the university, you may find applied sociologists working in government agencies, banks, manufacturing firms, and so forth.

Many sociologists have focused their attention on the methods and work of applied sociology, sometimes called "sociological practice." This interest, moreover, is truly global.

Mark van de Vall, at Erasmus University in Rotterdam, Netherlands, is a leading scholar in the practice of sociology. He has been interested particularly in the growing demand for policy-relevant sociological data.

> In satisfying this demand for usable knowledge, Sociology is going through a slow but steady process of professionalization. The emerging profession of "sociological practitioner" reflects three stages of policy making: 1. Diagnosing a policy problem; 2. Designing an alternative policy measure; 3. Developing a viable and feasible policy program. (van de Vall, 1992, p. 1)

Moving into more detail, van de Vall has diagrammed the specific steps involved in the application of sociology to social problems.

Starting Point
    1. a problem is felt

Sociologist as Diagnostician
    2. tentative diagnosis
    3. definitive diagnosis

Sociologist as Policy Adviser
    4. search for solutions
    5. determining priorities
    6. appraising solutions
    7. selecting one solution
    8. planning implementation
       a. stimulating awareness (cognitive)
       b. stimulating acceptance (affective)
       c. stimulating adjustment (behavioral)

Sociologist as Process Consultant
   9. implementing policy
  10. evaluation of policy
  11. revision of policy

Possible Outcomes
  12. institutionalization of policy
  13. termination of policy
  14. diffusion of policy to other organizations
        (van de Vall, 1992, p. 1a)

Van de Vall describes some of the settings in which such sociological policy research might be undertaken: regarding low-cost housing, health facilities, recreation, the location of new manufacturing plants, worker resources, or the needs of special populations, such as retarded persons, delinquents, immigrants, drug addicts, and so on. In truth, any aspect of society could reasonably be the focus for applied sociological research and policy formation.

Some of these activities are referred to more specifically as *evaluation research* or *program evaluation*. When you think about it, many of the activities of government and other organizations involve "interventions" intended to produce some result. It may start with a problem, such as student absenteeism in a school, and a program is designed to counteract it. Evaluation research is designed to determine whether the program had the intended effect.

In a bare bones format, the total programmed intervention would involve (a) the careful measurement of absenteeism at the outset, (b) the introduction of the new program—giving gold stars for perfect attendance, perhaps—and (c) the remeasurement of absenteeism afterward to see whether it had, in fact, been reduced. As logical as this procedure may seem, you might be surprised (and depressed) if you undertook to discover how many of our major social interventions are evaluated in this fashion. Typically (a) some people become concerned over what they believe to be a social problem, (b) someone has a "good idea" about how it might be solved, (c) the decision to go ahead is the result of political process, and (d) the success or failure of the program is never rigorously tested.

Many sociologists have expressed concern over the danger that sociological research findings are used within a primarily political process: cited by those whose personal opinions and preferences agree with the research, and dismissed out of hand by those who happen to disagree on nonscientific grounds. Thus, for example, at different times in history, sociological findings have been used to justify racial segregation in the United States (cited in *Plessy v. Ferguson*, 1896) and, later, to overturn it (cited in *Brown v. Board of Education of Topeka, Kansas*, 1954).

With this concern in mind, sociologists have looked specifically at ways sociologists can be more effective as technical experts. Michael I. Harrison, of Israel's Bar Ilan University, for example, writes about different consulting styles, paying attention to different sources of consultant power, different degrees of involvement in organizational politics, different processes for implementing organizational change, and the importance of whom consultants define as their clients (Harrison, 1991, pp. 92-107).

As you can see, the role of sociology in the arena of social policy and reform is potentially a full and powerful one. The "Reading Further" section at the end of this chapter suggests ways you can pursue your examination of this topic.

In the remainder of this chapter, however, I want to focus on one aspect of the general topic we've been discussing: the diagnosing of social problems. More specifically, we examine ways of determining the presence of *institutional discrimination*, because this is a topic of common concern. As we'll see, it is possible for social structure to be organized to produce discrimination based on race, gender, and other characteristics. Although the social structures in question may have been established by personally prejudiced people, we'll see that those structures continue to discriminate today, regardless of how the individual humans involved may feel about the discriminated-against groups. The method of determining the presence of institutional discrimination, however, is quite different from the way you might recognize discrimination in individuals.

Recall the discussion (in Chapter 2) of the Supreme Court's consideration of whether the disproportionate number of blacks suffering the death penalty was an indication of discrimination. The Court, as we saw, concluded that discrimination did not exist unless it could be found in the hearts and minds of the individuals involved. In this chapter, we will follow a different logic: one that lets us see the presence of discrimination within social structure, regardless of whether it can be found in the individual humans who comprise it.

Notice, as a simple example, that a rule requiring police officers to be at least 5 feet 8 inches tall would discriminate against women, in that women are, on the average, shorter than men. Thus the rule, as an element of social structure, would make fewer women than men eligible to be police officers. To the extent that different ethnic groups have different average heights, the same rule would discriminate in favor of some and against others. Such discrimination would be the case regardless of whether any of the police department recruiters or even the people who instituted the rule had discriminatory motives or were even prejudiced.

The plain fact is that the height rule is discriminatory with regard to gender and ethnicity. It would be counterproductive to describe the rule as prejudiced or bigoted, because such characteristics do not apply to social structure, only to human beings. Nonetheless the rule discriminates.

We may very well agree that such a rule—discriminating against women and some minorities, as it does—is still a good rule and should be maintained. Given the physical demands of police work, we might think that it is quite appropriate to have a minimum height standard.

It is worth noting that life is filled with discrimination: at the individual and social levels both. You and I discriminate all the time. You may discriminate in favor of "nice" people in choosing friends; you put all your money in banks, discriminating against strangers who offer to hold it on your behalf; you may have a preference for brain surgeons who have been to medical school, even further limiting your business to those who graduated and then went on to brain surgery school.

A good deal of discrimination also occurs at an organizational level. Banks prefer to lend money to people who are likely to pay it back; employers discriminate in favor of job seekers who seem able to do the work; convicted felons are not allowed to vote. (This latter is intended as a punishment, though half of those who are empowered to vote in the U.S. don't bother, somewhat lessening the sting of the punishment.)

As some of these examples suggest, discrimination is not necessarily "bad." Some instances of it seem perfectly logical and defensible even though we might disagree about some of the examples just given. In the discussions to follow, we will spend some time on whether specific grounds for institutional discrimination are justifiable, but most of our attention will focus on whether the patterns of discrimination that can be observed actually reflect those grounds alone or whether something more is involved.

THE SHIBBOLETH OF QUOTAS

In the early 1970s, concern over the persistence of racial and gender discrimination brought forth the idea of *affirmative action*, which suggested that employers had a responsibility to actively seek candidates from among minorities and women wherever those groups had been underemployed before. The Equal Employment Opportunities Act of 1972 established a commission to monitor compliance with affirmative action mandates. That was the source of the now-common statement "equal opportunity employer," and the employer was responsible for advertising jobs to draw the attention of minorities.

The philosophy behind affirmative action was that special steps needed to be taken to overcome the deeply ingrained patterns of discrimination built up over the course of centuries. It was no longer deemed sufficient for people to give up overt acts of discrimination, but each of us had a responsibility for taking positive steps—*affirmative* actions—to overthrow the legacy of the past.

Affirmative action has been linked frequently with the specter of "quotas" by those opposed to the program. This linkage has been accompanied by charges of "reverse discrimination"; in one celebrated case (*University of California Regents v. Bakke*, 1978), Alan Bakke, a young white man, successfully sued the University of California at Davis for excluding him from medical school as a result of a quota set aside for minorities. In one of its murkier decisions, the Supreme Court ruled in 1978 that affirmative action based on race was acceptable but that quotas were not. Some called the Court's decision "the lawyer's full-employment act."

In recent years, the phrase *level playing field* has been suggested by conservatives as a model of equal treatment today. The logic of this position is that (a) there was discrimination against minorities in the past and (b) there have been compensatory programs more recently, so now (c) everybody has an equal chance, with no special treatment for or against minorities.

Although the logic of the level playing field would seem to make sense, it ignores the depth to which racial and gender discrimination is embedded in the social structure. Suppose a young woman wants to be an aerospace engineer. In 1989, only 3.7% of all aerospace engineers in the U.S. were women (U.S. Bureau of the Census, 1991, p. 395). Here are just a few of the bumps in the aerospace engineering playing field for women.

- Few female role models for her to emulate
- All of her aerospace engineering professors—men
- Movies, books, and advertisements about aerospace engineers—all of them men

- Deep-seated belief that women are no good at math and science
- The economic threat women pose to a nearly all-male occupation
- A folk treasure of jokes about emotionality in women
- Religious injunctions about a woman's place being in the home
- Beliefs that women in male occupations are probably lesbians

The issue of quotas, then, arose in this context as a result of the need for a method to evaluate whether employers really were taking affirmative actions or simply were going through the motions. In short, the only real evidence that the aerospace industry is really opening up to female engineers is if more women became aerospace engineers. Hence the numbers of women and ethnic minorities in various occupations, industries, and organizations have become an important indicator of discrimination or the lack of it. Implicitly there must be *some* percentage of representation that would indicate a lack of discrimination. However, specifying the appropriate number would constitute the specification of the quota.

Even in the case of the level playing field, it is difficult to assess whether discrimination exists. Fortunately some sociological research techniques lend themselves readily to the solution of this problem. The next section continues the examination of discrimination and introduces you to multivariate analysis.

THE LOGIC OF MULTIVARIATE ANALYSIS

As a simple example of how it is possible to identify discrimination, imagine that a police department has a height requirement of 5 feet 6 inches. Imagine further that 50% of the city's population are women. If we were unaware of the gender difference in height, we would expect reasonably that half of the police officers should be women.

Because women are, on average, shorter than men, let's assume that 40% of all of those 5 feet 6 inches or taller in the population are women. If there were no sex discrimination per se, we would expect that 40%—not 50%—of the police officers should be women. If women comprised a smaller proportion of the force—let's say, 20%—that would suggest, but not prove, that women are being discriminated against *as women*.

Take a moment now to think of other factors that might account for the smaller proportion of women on the police force. What would be another explanation for the "shortage" of women that would not involve the system or anyone involved in it actually discriminating against women directly? Once you've thought about this yourself, continue reading.

As you reflected on this matter, you may have wondered whether women were as likely as men to *apply* for jobs as police officers. In the extreme, suppose that no women applied; then the police force would automatically, and reasonably, be all male.

A better test for the presence of discrimination on the basis of gender per se, then, should build on the percentage of women among the *applicants* who were at least 5 feet 6 inches tall. If the percentage of women accepted onto the police force was less than their percentage among qualified (by height) applicants, then we would be justified in suspecting sex discrimination.

In sociological research, a technique called *multivariate analysis* allows for an examination of the impact of several factors (variables) in determining outcomes. Typically this approach is used to explain how individual humans turn out: whether they are liberal or conservative, religious or not, rich or poor, and so forth. The same logic can be used to detect discrimination at the level of social structure.

Multivariate analysis operates on the logic of *causal explanation*. It seeks to determine what factors cause specific outcomes. Thus, in the case of political outlooks, mentioned above, we might ask what influence was exerted by such variables as parents' political outlooks, region of the country, education, occupation, social class, and so forth. Each of these factors would be found to have some influence on whether individuals were liberal or conservative, and different statistical techniques allow us to assess the relative importance of each.

Given the nature of human behavior, it is seldom, if ever, possible to account totally for such qualities of political outlook, religiosity, or the other kinds of characteristics sociologists study. There is always some degree of what we call *unexplained variance*, which serves the dual functions of keeping sociologists humble and assuring people that they are not totally determined but enjoy some degree of free will.

The use of this analytical model for the purpose of detecting institutional discrimination works as follows. First, we begin with the position that discrimination exists whenever a subgroup of society (e.g., women, Hispanics) are underrepresented in a particular position (on police forces, getting bank loans, etc.) as compared with their percentage in the total population. Thus, if women are 50% of a city's population and only 30% of its police force, this is taken as prima facie evidence of institutional discrimination. If the result is unrepresentative, then the system discriminates.

Second, we must identify *legitimate* grounds for discrimination. We might agree, for example, that height is a legitimate ground for discrimination. Perhaps we would agree that differences in the rates with which people apply for jobs is a legitimate explanation for differences in how they are represented among those selected. Neither of these explanations is necessarily the case, however.

The height requirement, for example, might be justified in the case of police officers in the front lines of confronting violent crime, but not all police jobs involve that. Probably height is not a relevant requirement for answering the telephone, filing records, and any number of other jobs required by a police department. Thus it might be appropriate to limit an analysis to a smaller arena than initially imagined.

If men are more likely than women to apply for police jobs, that is not necessarily an excuse for unrepresentative outcomes. It may be appropriate to examine the reasons for differential rates of applying for jobs, loans, and so on. It is commonly the case that established patterns of discrimination will result in those discriminated against giving up. If you reach the conclusion that "people like you" never get hired at ABC Company, you are unlikely to go to the trouble of applying. The logic of multivariate analysis, however, allows a determination of whether social structure is discriminatory in generating attempts at participation. We can determine, for example, whether the rate at which women apply for police jobs is the same as the proportion who are over 5 feet 6 inches tall. If fewer apply than the height difference would suggest, we can conclude that the system discriminates in some manner other than the height requirement.

As we'll see in the following examples, the logic of multivariate analysis could be marshalled to detect any chilling effects due to past patterns of institutional functioning. It is important to separate the existence of de facto discrimination from the affective qualities of humans, such as prejudice, bigotry, and ill-will. If women are disproportionately unlikely to apply for police jobs, it may be due to any number of factors that may be the "fault" of male chauvinism, the system, or the women themselves; but the point is that a pattern of discrimination exists—whatever its cause.

Topics such as these are so emotional for humans that it is essential to keep the determination of discrimination separate from discussion of why it exists. Although it is possible to research the causes, it is essential

Table 7.1. **Average Annual Income of Men and Women in Executive and Clerical Jobs**

	Men	Women	Proportion Women/Men
Executives	$36,696	$21,551	59%
Clerical	$19,991	$16,539	83%

SOURCE: Data are from Statistical Abstract of the United States (p. 417) by U.S. Bureau of the Census, 1991, Washington, DC: Government Printing Office.

to address its existence as a separate matter. Otherwise the analysis of observable patterns becomes hopelessly entangled with human prejudices, preferences, and predispositions.

GENDER AND SALARIES

In 1989, the average male full-time salaried worker in the U.S. earned $468 per week. His female counterpart earned 70% as much: $328 (U.S. Bureau of the Census, 1991, p. 415). Is this a matter of discrimination? Some have argued that it is not, offering legitimate reasons for the difference in terms of other variables.

It also is argued that women earn less than men because they tend to work in occupations that have lower average incomes: nurses rather than doctors, secretaries rather than bosses, and so on. Let's look at this possibility.

The differences in types of jobs would seem to be borne out by the data, shown in Table 7.1. For example, women constitute only 59% of the workers in the census category "executive, administrator, and managerial," whereas they are 83% of the workers in the category "administrative, support, including clerical." This discrepancy could account for the differences between men and women, but it doesn't. No matter which of these categories women work in, they earn substantially less than men.

Another explanation offered for women's lower incomes is that they are more likely to work part-time or to work only part of the year. Because the data just presented represent all workers in the two categories considered, perhaps this explains the differences. The data in Table 7.2 are limited to year-round, full-time workers.

Table 7.2. Average Annual Income of Men and Women in Executive and Clerical Jobs, Year-Round Full-Time Workers Only

	Men	Women	Proportion Women/Men
Executives	$40,103	$24,589	61%
Clerical	$25,138	$17,517	70%

SOURCE: *Data are from* Statistical Abstract of the United States (*p. 417*) *by U.S. Bureau of the Census, 1991, Washington, DC: Government Printing Office.*

This new variable fails to account for the gender difference in incomes. In fact, full-time year-round male clerical workers earn more than full-time year-round female executives.

It is argued sometimes that men are more likely to be the primary earner for a family and hence it is more likely that they will place themselves in higher paying jobs—or else they couldn't support their families. Let's see.

In 1989, more than 9 million married-couple families in the U.S. had one breadwinner: the husband. These husbands earned an average of $502 per week. More than 2 million families were supported by only the wife, and they had an average weekly income of $251. Thus, when the variable "number of earners in the family" is controlled for, women earn only half as much as men (U.S. Bureau of the Census, 1991, p. 416).

A similar picture is found when we consider single-parent families. About 2 million such families were headed by men in 1989, and more than 7 million were headed by women. Regardless of whether the head of household was the only earner or others chipped in, the families headed by women did worse, as is shown in Table 7.3.

Notice that, in some of these analyses, we have been controlling for more than one variable at a time. For example, we compared men and women while holding occupational level and full-time status constant. Any gender differences left over when those variables are held constant must be due to something else: either other "legitimate" factors or discrimination.

A more sophisticated analysis would be one that held all such variables constant at once. One such study was conducted by researchers at the University of Michigan. Levitin, Quinn, and Staines (1971) under-

Table 7.3. Average Weekly Income of Single-Parent Families

| | Families headed by | | Proportion |
	Men	Women	Women/Men
One earner	$382	$347	91%
Two or more earners	$718	$566	79%

SOURCE: Data are from Statistical Abstract of the United States (p. 416) by U.S. Bureau of the Census, 1991, Washington, DC: Government Printing Office.

took to consider all of the variables that legitimately might affect how much money a person earned.

They began with the data from a national survey of both male and female workers. First, they separated the men and women in the data; then, they divided the men into two groups at random. In one of the groups, they undertook a *regression* analysis designed to create an equation for predicting income. The researchers considered such variables as occupation, years of work experience, education and other training, and many other relevant factors. The data at hand allowed them to consider just about any variable you might think of as legitimately affecting income.

Working with half of the male cases, the researchers had the computer construct an equation that best predicted the incomes of the men being studied. Once the equation was created, the researchers used it to predict the incomes of the other men in the study: those who had not been considered in the construction of the equation. This was a test of whether the equation really predicted income or was simply an artifact of the first set of men analyzed.

The equation predicted the incomes of the other men within $30 per year! In short, it offered an excellent summary of all of the factors affecting pay, showing how much influence each factor had, and indicating how much a person with a particular set of characteristics should earn.

Then the researchers applied the same equation to the women in the study. They overestimated women's incomes by an average of $3,000 per year. In other words, a woman with all of the same characteristics as a man would earn, on average, $3,000 less. The implication of this analysis is that even when all of the legitimate reasons for paying people more or less were taken into account, the residual cost of discrimination against women amounted to $3,000 per year.

Let's consider another example to illustrate how the logic of multivariate analysis can be used to identify instances of institutional discrimination.

RACE AND CAPITAL PUNISHMENT

In Chapter 2, I mentioned the Supreme Court's denial that capital punishment is racially discriminatory. In this section, I look more deeply into the data, using a multivariate analysis. Samuel R. Gross and Robert Mauro (1989) set the stage for this discussion.

> Of 3,984 people lawfully executed since 1930 [through 1987], 2,113 were black, over half of the total and almost five times the proportion of blacks in the population as a whole. But this disproportion, while striking, does not demonstrate that there has been racial discrimination in the administration of the death penalty. The great majority of death sentences since 1930 have been imposed for homicide, and the black homicide rate in that period has been several times higher than the white homicide rate. The disparity in death sentences and executions could simply reflect the disparity in homicides. (p. 17)

To elaborate on the authors' reference to black and white homicide rates, we might note that although blacks make up about 12% of the U.S. population at present (U.S. Bureau of the Census, 1991, p. 38), 54.7% of those arrested for murder and nonnegligent manslaughter in 1990 were black, as were 48.6% of murder victims (Federal Bureau of Investigation [FBI], 1990, pp. 11, 192). In stark contrast, only 3.2% of lawyers and judges are black, as are only 7.3% of all sheriffs, bailiffs, and other law enforcement officers (U.S. Bureau of the Census, 1991, pp. 395, 397).

Clearly blacks and whites are not equal in these respects. Whites disproportionately run the criminal justice system, and blacks are disproportionately punished by it. If blacks constituted 12% of the law enforcement professions, 12% of the victims, and 12% of the offenders, then we would assume that race was irrelevant to this subject. Clearly it is not irrelevant.

Many points of debate surround these matters. It is alleged, for example, that blacks are more likely to be falsely arrested and wrongly convicted once arrested. In contrast to the data on gender and income, there is an element of doubt in data on crime and punishment. If we want to know how much someone earns in a year, we can simply ask that person, and on the whole we can take what he or she tells us as data for our analyses. When the court asks a defendant whether he or she committed the murder in question, however, we don't take that answer as necessarily being the truth. And even if a person is convicted of murder, that's not a certainty either, because innocent people are sometimes convicted.

In this discussion, however, we will focus on a specific aspect of the criminal justice system: capital punishment. The question is whether blacks are discriminated against by the death penalty.

By way of historical background, the Supreme Court outlawed all capital punishment in 1972 in the case of *Furman v. Georgia.* The reason for the action was a bit unclear, reflecting the different reasoning of the justices who voted with the majority. Some thought the death penalty was cruel and unusual punishment; others thought its application was arbitrary. Justice Brennan likened it to a lottery system. Justice Marshall, the first black justice on the Supreme Court, thought that the data available to the court indicated that capital punishment discriminated against blacks and against the poor more generally. Four years later, the Court reversed its position in *Gregg v. Georgia* (1976) and ruled that several newly written death penalty statues were constitutional. Soon the nation's death rows were repopulated, and prisoners again were being executed.

In 1987, the Supreme Court heard another landmark case, *McCleskey v. Kemp* (1987), which argued that blacks were discriminated against in the application of the death penalty. As I indicated in Chapter 2, the Court did not contest the data submitted but denied that they represented racial discrimination. In the remainder of this section, I review some of the data presented because they illustrate the kind of multivariate analysis that is the subject of this chapter.

The focus of this analysis rests on the fact that most of those convicted of murder are *not* sentenced to death: roughly only 1 in 100. The question is whether race is involved in the decision of whether or not those convicted are given the death penalty. Gross and Mauro (1989) focused their analyses on three states—Georgia, Florida, and Illinois—the states that had amassed the largest number of death sentences during the period under study.

The initial analysis would suggest that charges of racial discrimination against blacks are completely unfounded. Indeed, in the three states mentioned, whites convicted of murder were substantially more likely to get the death penalty than were blacks (see Table 7.4)!

Table 7.4. Percentage of Whites and Blacks Sentenced to Death, Data From Three States

	Georgia	*Florida*	*Illinois*
Whites	5.5	5.2	1.8
Blacks	2.9	2.4	1.5

SOURCE: *Adapted from* Death and Discrimination: Racial Disparities in Capital Sentencing *(p. 44) by S. R. Gross & R. Mauro, 1989, Boston: Northeastern.*

The logic of multivariate analysis involves the identification of variables that can help explain the relationship between two other variables. In this case, the original two variables are the race of the convicted murders and the likelihood of their receiving the death penalty. Can you guess the third variable that can shed light on the original relationship?

The *race of the victim* holds the key in this case. As we shall see, most murders are black-on-black or white-on-white, and the race of the murder victim has a powerful effect on whether or not murderers are sentenced to the death penalty. First, let's look at the relationship between race of victim and race of murderer. To simplify, in Table 7.5 I've combined the data from the three states under study.

As Table 7.5 indicates, most murders are within, rather than between, races. Notice also that although blacks are in the minority within the population, more of them are murdered than whites. Therefore the *likelihood* of a black person being killed is much higher than for whites.

Table 7.5. Relationship Between Race of Murder Victim and Race of Murderer, Combined Data From Three States

		Race of Victim	
		White	*Black*
	White	83%	3%
Race of defendant			
	Black	17%	97%
	100% =	(3,762)	(5,366)

SOURCE: *Calculated from data in* Death and Discrimination: Racial Disparities in Capital Sentencing *(p. 45) by S. R. Gross & R. Mauro, 1989, Boston: Northeastern.*

Table 7.6. Percentage of White and Black Murderers Sentenced to Death, Data From Three States

Race of Victim	Georgia	Florida	Illinois
White	8.7%	6.3%	2.9%
Black	0.9%	0.8%	0.5%

SOURCE: *Adapted from* Death and Discrimination: Racial Disparities in Capital Sentencing *(p. 44) by S. R. Gross &* R. Mauro, 1989, Boston: Northeastern.

In each of the three states under study, the likelihood of a person being sentenced to death for killing a white person is far greater than if the victim is black (see Table 7.6).

Race of the victim, then, accounts for the fact that whites are more likely to be sentenced to death—because they are more likely to kill white victims. Table 7.7 examines all three variables simultaneously. Again, for simplicity, I've combined the three states.

As we see in these data, the race of the victim has a strong impact on whether the defendant is sentenced to death. Moreover, when blacks kill whites, the likelihood of a death sentence is far greater than in any of the other possibilities. The very low rate of capital punishment in the case of blacks killing blacks has been alleged to represent a view that violence within the black community isn't all that significant to the larger community.

Table 7.7. Percentage of White and Black Murderers Sentenced to Death, Data From Three States, Combined Variables

		Race of Victim	
		White	Black
	White	4.3%	2.5%
Race of defendant			
	Black	13.2%	0.7%
	100% =	(3,762)	(5,366)

SOURCE: *Calculated from data in* Death and Discrimination: Racial Disparities in Capital Sentencing *(p. 45) by S. R. Gross &* R. Mauro, 1989, Boston: Northeastern.

**Table 7.8. Percentage of Murderers Sentenced to Death,
Single Versus Multiple Victims**

Single Victim:		Race of Victim	
		White	Black
Race of defendant	White	3.5%	2.5%
	Black	11.7%	0.5%

Multiple Victims:		Race of Victims	
		White	Black
Race of defendant	White	18.9%	*
	Black	35.9%	8.0%

NOTE: *Too few cases for a meaningful percentage.*
SOURCE: *Calculated from data in* Death and Discrimination: Racial Disparities
in Capital Sentencing *(p. 45) by S. R. Gross &
R. Mauro, 1989, Boston: Northeastern.*

When Gross and Mauro (1989) took account of whether a particular homicide involved a single victim or multiple victims, the racial effect became even clearer, as presented in Table 7.8.

Gross and Mauro (1989) extended their analyses further to include several other variables that legitimately might influence whether death sentences were handed out: whether the homicide occurred in the commission of another felony, whether the killer and victim were strangers or knew each other, the gender of the victim, what weapons were used in the homicides, the rural or urban location of the crime, and the number of aggravating circumstances involved in the crime. To accommodate the large number of variables, the authors employed regression techniques similar to those described above in the case of gender and salary.

All of the analyses pointed to two consistent conclusions. First, the application of the death penalty grossly discounts the importance of black victims; it is far more likely if the victim is white. Second, the death penalty is by far most likely to be given in the case of blacks killing whites.

When the Supreme Court reviewed the mass of data submitted on the discriminatory manner in which the death penalty was applied in Georgia, they accepted the research, saying, "We assume the study is valid statistically." However, they refused to take the data as evidence of racial discrimination, asserting that statistical evidence per se was "insufficient to support an inference that any of the decision makers in McCleskey's case acted with discriminatory purpose" (quoted in Gross & Mauro, 1989, p. 160). In other words, the Court ruled out altogether the concept of *institutional discrimination*. Presumably the only persuasive evidence would have been confessions from jurors that they had voted for the death penalty simply because the defendant was black.

This example illustrates the manner in which multivariate analysis can be used to identify instances of discrimination. It also illustrates the fact that the subjects sociologists study are often matters of ingrained belief and emotion, and the implications of scientific findings are not automatically acted on.

BANK LOANS

One more short example should complete your understanding of the logic that has so far escaped the justices of the Supreme Court. It sometimes is alleged that banks discriminate against minority loan applicants. The bank officers, for their part, respond that they make their decisions on a purely business basis. Although I do not have data to use in an actual analysis of this matter, let's see how such an analysis might be undertaken.

First, we would need to identify all of the variables that would be regarded as "legitimate" bases for the granting or refusal of loans. Examples of such variables might include value of assets, employment status and employment history, past loan-payment history, and purpose of the loan.

If the research were being conducted within the arena of public debate, we would aim to get both sides to agree on the set of legitimate variables. Probably we would ask representatives of the banks to indicate what they regarded as legitimate variables, and we would see whether representatives from the aggrieved minority groups concurred.

For the sake of simplicity, let's begin by considering two variables: (a) whether the loan applicants are employed currently and (b) whether they have ever declared bankruptcy. We then would collect data on all

Table 7.9. Hypothetical Data on Minority Versus Majority Bank Loan Applications, Two Variables

Percent approved:		Minority Applicant		Majority Applicant	
	Employed?	Yes	No	Yes	No
Bankruptcy in the past?	Yes	20%	0%	20%	0%
	No	80%	30%	80%	30%

loan applicants over some designated period of time: the two variables just mentioned, applicants' ethnicity, and whether the loan was approved. These data could be analyzed in a table like Table 7.9.

These hypothetical data tell us several things. First, they confirm that the banks base their loans largely on the "legitimate" variables under consideration. Employed applicants are much more likely to have their loans approved than are the unemployed. Moreover, those with past bankruptcies are at a definite disadvantage.

These hypothetical data also suggest that the banks did not discriminate on the basis of ethnicity because minority and majority applicants had the same success rates in getting loans—when the "legitimate" discriminatory variables were taken into account and held constant.

In a real analysis of this issue, there would, no doubt, be several variables to consider. As we've seen in the two preceding examples, statistical techniques—such as regression analysis—can handle more complicated analyses than are feasible with simple percentage tables.

Before concluding this discussion, we need to look at another aspect of such multivariate analyses. In real analyses, the data seldom are as neat as those shown in Table 7.9. The final question remaining is, How much of a difference really makes a difference? How much discrepancy in the loan rates of minority and majority applicants would be needed for us to conclude that the results were a sign of discrimination?

STATISTICAL SIGNIFICANCE

Several years ago, I found myself in the unpleasant position of being charged (as a department chair) with sex discrimination in hiring faculty.

The charge was brought against the department by an unhappy woman who had applied for a job and had not gotten it.

The allegation of discrimination actually had three parts. The first allegation was that we discriminated in favor of people with Ph.D.s, which she lacked. In the subsequent hearings, I pleaded us guilty in that regard, and the hearing board acknowledged that we were perfectly justified in using that criteria in the selection of university faculty because one of the tasks of faculty was to supervise students who were working for Ph.D.s.

The second allegation was that a Zionist clique within our department discriminated against Palestinians, which was her background. This was a more serious charge, in my mind, and it was an uncomfortable one to address. When the panel asked me how many of the faculty were Jewish, I indicated that because we didn't require them to wear yellow arm bands, it was difficult to know. When the plaintiff identified the three Zionists who supposedly ran the department, however, I was able to report that only one of the three was even Jewish and that I didn't think he would consider himself a Zionist.

The third allegation of discrimination was, I felt, more legitimate: The department discriminated against women. In a department faculty of 20 professors, only 2 were women. On the face of it, these numbers seemed to suggest a pattern of discrimination.

Although the panel concluded that we were justified in not hiring the candidate, who lacked a Ph.D., I personally was concerned about the possibility that a pattern of sex discrimination might exist nonetheless. Because I've discussed the analyses I undertook in this regard elsewhere (Babbie, 1988, pp. 112-117), I will only summarize here.

The presence of only 2 women among 20 faculty, on the face of it, seemed to hint at sex discrimination because, implicitly, it would seem as though half should be women. However, substantially fewer than half the Ph.D. sociologists in the nation were women at the time. So the question became one of how many women faculty would be expected if there were no discrimination operating over the years and how we would determine that was the case.

Initially I examined our most recent hiring history, during the time I had been chair. During those most recent years, we had quite good records of all of the people who had applied for faculty positions, who had received offers from us, and who actually had accepted our offers and been employed. Because we could determine people's gender from their names in almost all cases, I was able to examine our pattern of offers and hires.

Overall, I found the department, in recent years, had made more offers to women candidates than would have been expected from their proportion among all candidates. So, if 30% of the applicants were women, say, 50% of the offers we made were to women. However, not all of those to whom we offered jobs accepted. On balance, however, in the most recent years, the proportion of women among those hired was approximately the same as the proportion of women among the applicants.

I was convinced that the department had not engaged in a pattern of sex discrimination in recent years, which was comforting, but what about the longer haul? Perhaps the department had not been as egalitarian in the years prior to the national concern for sexual equality. Notice that this inquiry required us to consider the department as an entity rather than the individual faculty because none of us had been on the faculty throughout its whole history.

To explore this possibility, I examined the hiring of each of the 20 faculty who served in the department at that time. There were no records of the manner in which they were hired—data on the competing applicants, for example—so I had to make some approximations about whom they might have been competing with. Specifically I analyzed their national cohort of Ph.D. recipients as their most probable competitors.

For example, I had received my Ph.D. in 1969. I made the assumption that I had been chosen from among other candidates who were more or less like me, at least in terms of relative seniority in the field. For purposes of the analysis, therefore, I assumed I had been chosen from among all of those others who had received their degrees in 1969. National statistics indicated that 20% of those of us who received Ph.D.s in sociology that year were women.

To test for sex discrimination, it was necessary to establish what nondiscrimination would look like. Perhaps the clearest model was that of *random selection*. If faculty were selected at random, then we would have hired the proper proportion of men and women—equal to their proportions among the applicant pools.

For analytical purposes, therefore, I simulated the random selection model by saying that when I was hired, a totally nondiscriminatory process would have hired 0.80 men and 0.20 women because that was the proportion in the total applicant pool. Although this fiction made no sense in the case of hiring a single faculty member, it was a useful device for analyzing a history of hiring.

Another of the faculty, a woman, also received her degree in 1969. The nondiscriminatory, random selection model, again, would have hired 0.80 men and 0.20 women. Adding our two cases, the random model would suggest a total of 1.60 men and 0.40 women. In fact, of course, we represented one of each.

I repeated this process for all of the 20 faculty, adding up all of the portions of men and women that a random selection process would have hired over the years. Such a process would have hired three women, not two. Now the question was whether that was proof of discrimination by the department as a social entity.

To assess this issue, it is necessary to recognize that random selection processes do not produce exactly predictable results. If you were to flip a coin 100 times, for example, you'd expect to get half heads and half tails—but not exactly half. You might very well get 51 heads and 49 tails or 48 heads and 52 tails. Neither of those outcomes would cause you to question whether you had a "fair" coin. If you got 100 heads and no tails, on the other hand, you could be pretty sure something was wrong with the coin. (At least, you should avoid betting against the person who owns the coin.)

Random selection is a part of what statisticians refer to as *probability theory*. In such processes, different outcomes have different probabilities of occurring. Thus 51 heads out of 100 is much more probable than 100 heads out of 100. When sociologists look for patterns of social behavior, they often use the probability theory model as a device for testing whether something they've observed represents a genuine social regularity or could be just a result of chance. Thus if one particular physician in a large clinic earns only half as much as a particular white physician, that could easily be a function of chance—due to the particular physicians we happened to examine. If a random sample of 1,000 black physicians earns an average of half as much as a random sample of 1,000 white physicians in a city, however, that's more significant. In fact, statisticians speak of *statistical significance* in this regard. It is very unlikely that such a difference would occur by chance only, and it would seem likely that racial discrimination was operating.

Here's a simple illustration of such probabilities. Let's return to flipping coins. Suppose you were to flip a coin four times. How many heads would you expect to get? If you answered two, that's a sensible response. You stand a better chance of getting two heads than any other number, but actually your chances of getting *exactly* two aren't as good as you might think. That's apparent when you examine all of the possibilities, shown in Table 7.10.

Table 7.10. Possible Outcomes of Flipping a Coin Four Times

Flips 1 2 3 4	No. of Heads
H H H H	4
H H H T	3
H H T H	3
H T H H	3
T H H H	3
H H T T	2
H T H T	2
H T T H	2
T H T H	2
T H H T	2
T T H H	2
H T T T	1
T H T T	1
T T H T	1
T T T H	1
T T T T	0

Of the 16 possible outcomes, 6 have two heads. Although that's the most common outcome, it occurs only 37.5% of the time. Looked at differently, the odds are almost 2 to 1 *against* your getting two heads. Thus, if you were to perform this experiment and get only one head or get three, you would have no reason to imagine that something was wrong with the coin. In fact, you could get four heads or no heads and not suspect the coin.

Now imagine you did the same experiment but increased the number of flips to 100. Now the range of possibilities has expanded dramatically: from 0 heads to 100 heads. I won't try to present the list of possible outcomes because there would be 10,000 in this expanded experiment. If you wrote out the list for yourself, you'd discover that the most common outcome was still a 50/50 split: with 5,000 heads and 5,000 tails. The likelihood of getting *exactly* half heads, however, is even smaller than before: about 1 in 125. The likelihood of getting either all heads or all tails is virtually nil: 1 in 10,000 in either case. If you were to flip a coin

100 times and get all heads, you might want to check to be sure that there's a tail on one side.

Sociological research often takes advantage of a similar body of probability statistics. It is often possible to determine whether it is likely that an observed pattern could have happened just by chance or whether it represents something real in social life. And, as we've seen, in the simple example of gender and faculty hiring, that same logic can distinguish patterns of discrimination from chance variations.

CONCLUSION

The purpose of the techniques discussed in this chapter is to find ways of identifying characteristics of social structure. When an individual speaks disparagingly of a minority ethnic group, it's easy to recognize that as prejudice. And when such an individual refuses to hire members of particular groups, that's a clear case of discrimination.

This book is devoted to understanding a different level of reality, made up of social structure rather than individuals. As we've seen, it is possible for social structure to produce discrimination even in the absence of what we think of as prejudice. In fact, it would be possible to create a system, structured with particular constraints, and it would produce certain results regardless of the kind of people who participate in that system. It is worth noting that former Secretary of Defense Robert McNamara commissioned what were to become the infamous "Pentagon papers" in an effort to discover how a group of highly intelligent people, committed to staying out of a land war in Asia, could have gotten involved in one anyway.

Because social structure is so different from human beings, special tools are needed to understand it. The sociological diagnostic techniques discussed in this chapter are some of those that are appropriate to understanding social structure and recognizing its problems.

Points of Discussion

- What other problems of discrimination do you think might be studied in the manner described in this chapter?

- How might the techniques described in this chapter be used to determine whether the federal government was distributing highway funds to states on the basis of need or on the basis of political deal making?

- How might these techniques be used to discover the bases on which the U.S. government grants foreign aid to other countries?

Reading Further

For a further discussion of multivariate analysis, consider my textbook *The Practice of Social Research* (Belmont, CA: Wadsworth, 1992). Another source of numerous illustrations is Morris Rosenberg's *The Logic of Survey Research* (New York: Basic Books, 1968).

A classic example of the use of social statistics to identify and understand social problems can be found in Emile Durkheim's *Suicide* (New York: Free Press, 1897/1951). Working with regional suicide rates, Durkheim demonstrated a logic of associating the rates with other characteristics of the regions (predominant religions, for example) to offer sound speculations about the motivations of the individuals committing suicide.

Morton Hunt's *Profiles of Social Research: The Scientific Study of Human Interactions* (New York: Russell Sage, 1985) chronicles a number of sociological studies that have had an impact on society.

CHAPTER EIGHT

Taking Charge

My purpose in this book has been to introduce you to some sociological notions that can empower you in your dealings with society. Most specifically, I've wanted to alert you to the ways social structures we create often take on lives of their own—that's a fundamental aspect of how we create them—and soon we are serving them rather than the way we intended. Once alerted to the way things are, you should be in a better position to deal with social structure more powerfully. Perhaps you'll find yourself taking on the task of changing structures that are no longer appropriate.

Perhaps, just perhaps, you will find yourself joining the ranks of sociologists, realizing that this is where the action will be for the foreseeable future. There's plenty of work to be done and plenty of room for people who feel up to the challenge that lies ahead.

In this final chapter, I want to suggest some of the directions that sociology will follow in the next few decades. Throughout its history, sociology has acted on two major agenda: scientific inquiry and social action. During different periods of time, the profession has given one or the other more emphasis, but the two agenda have been interrelated. The scientific findings derived from objective research activities have been useful to those more interested in social reform, and concerns for social action have often helped focus research activities.

Let's take a moment to look at what topics are likely to be researched and acted on in the years to come.

TOPICS FOR RESEARCH AND ACTION

From the beginning, American sociological interest in social action has focused primarily on matters of social justice, with countless studies of prejudice and discrimination, poverty, and so on. Although it will seem perhaps obvious and desirable, it is worth pointing out that sociologists have been just about unanimous in opposing prejudice, whether based on race, religion, gender, or other grounds. Moreover, studies of poverty have aimed implicitly at easing the suffering of the poor.

I point out these orientations because there are other logical possibilities. Specifically sociology as a discipline could have been devoted to the maintenance and protection of the ruling class. We might have studied poverty, for example, for the purpose of finding ways to keep the poor in their place, to prevent them from seeking to improve their lot, and so on. Note that this was an allegation Karl Marx (1875) lodged against the churches, saying religion was "the opiate of the masses." In his view, the churches persuaded the poor to accept their lot in this life, believing they would be rewarded in the afterlife. Regardless of whether or to what extent Marx's criticism of religion was justified, it would not be an accurate assessment of the role played by sociology and sociologists in America.

It seems obvious to me that sociology will continue to focus on topics of social justice in the years ahead. As I mention in Chapter 7, moreover, sociology has a set of analytical tools that are ideally suited to the discovery and documentation of discrimination. These tools allow the matter to be addressed in a scientifically objective manner, rather than through emotional charge and countercharge. It is clear, nonetheless, that the general public and government figures must be educated in the logic of the techniques discussed.

In the years to come, it also seems likely that sociologists will turn more attention to issues relating to the environment. During the environmentally active 1970s, the general public developed a basic, albeit reluctant, acceptance of the need to take care of our planet, and certain values—against littering and polluting, for example—that now make a more effective social movement possible as we prepare to address the hole in the ozone layer, global warming, and similar environmental challenges.

The need to confront environmental problems has been dramatized further by a better understanding of pollution in Eastern Europe, kept from view during the Soviet era but now open to view. Ironically these environmental problems are being addressed at a time when the cessation of cold war hostilities potentially frees hundreds of billions of dollars previously spent annually on preparations for war. The shift from military to environmental uses will not happen automatically or easily, but it is possible.

Sociologists are in a position to deal with whole systems involving the wide range of factors that must be interrelated in dealing with such grand issues. Economic factors alone will not work. Values are not the only answer. Politics will be involved, but politics is not sufficient. The problem has social and psychological dimensions, but such matters are insufficient in and of themselves. Again, sociology, as you've seen in this book, is the discipline best suited to integrating all such issues. I am not suggesting that we currently know everything necessary for the successful prosecution of the environmental campaign required for long-term survival, but sociology is the place to look for the answers that will work.

Sociologists have been involved in environmental concerns—both as scientists and as citizen-activists—in the past, but it seems to me that this area will become far more prominent in the years ahead. One aspect of this general topic deserves special attention: population.

HOW CAN YOU USE WHAT YOU'VE LEARNED?

Finally let's reflect on what the preceding discourse may mean to you. How do any of the discussions earlier in the book affect you? First, the sociological perspective can empower you to deal with a wide range of personal interests: getting into college, getting out, getting a job, getting promoted, finding a mate, and so forth. You should have learned some things in the preceding chapters that will help you deal more effectively with a college administration, department of motor vehicles, or bank loan department.

Second, you should have become more potent in dealing with the many social problems that beset our society and planet. I certainly don't mean to suggest what problems should concern you. Deciding what warrants your time and good efforts is probably as important as the work itself. I do hope that you will find some social problems that engage your concern and time.

Here are some suggestions that may assist you in dealing with problematic social structure either on your own behalf or on behalf of others.

Always Distinguish Organizations From Individuals

Here is a paradox. As you proceed to take on various personal troubles and social problems, I offer you two seemingly contradictory pieces of advice. First, if you find yourself talking about organizations acting (e.g., "The college says that you must . . . "), remind yourself that organizations don't act. They don't think, they don't feel, and they don't act. Those are things human beings do. So, if you want to make an organization stop doing something, look for the individual humans, who are really the ones feeling, thinking, and acting.

Second, whenever you find yourself blaming an individual for some social problem (e.g., "The president insists on appointing pond scum . . ."), ask yourself whether the situation that troubles you may not be the product of social structure. Quite possibly, a saint would behave the same way as the person who's bothering you, if placed in the same social circumstance.

The purpose of the first advice is to give you someone to talk to, who can do something about the situation you face. You can't talk to IBM, the telephone company, or Congress. You can talk to individuals, however, and you may even get them to change their ways.

The purpose of the second advice is to encourage detachment and compassion. Sometimes you can work more effectively when you can look at things objectively, taking your feelings out of the drama. Also you probably will be more persuasive with people if you can approach them from the point of view that they may be doing the best they can. Maybe you'd do the same in their shoes, and maybe you'd be as blind as they seem to be, given their position. Just as you'd want others to work with you instead of against you, that's not a bad place to invoke the Golden Rule.

In Chapter 1, I talked about The Holiday Project, a volunteer organization that has individuals visit shut-ins during the Christmas and Hanukkah holidays each year. I have the advantage of having participated as a volunteer who went along with a group visiting a hospital or retirement home, I've been responsible for organizing such a visit, and I've participated in various other ways, including a number of years on the national board of directors.

In my earlier discussion, I talked about the several ways in which such organizations seem to get off-purpose, devoting more and more of their time and energies (and often their budgets) to administrative matters, rather than to the activities around which they were originally formed. Very often, the different parts of a single organization will get involved in a struggle against one another, despite the fact that all of the individuals are committed to the same end result.

What I am describing here is true of private voluntary associations, government agencies, and private profit-making companies. I like examining the problem in the case of voluntary associations, however, because so many factors—like making a living, getting ahead—are not present to complicate matters. Although individual human motives and emotions are not absent certainly, they are less of a factor. Also, in voluntary associations, you typically are dealing with individuals who have and operate from pure motives. Thus problems that arise cannot easily be attributed to "bad people."

In the case of The Holiday Project, I often found myself and my fellow directors complaining about "the local committees" and their failures to abide by the organizational agreements. From our vantage point, we could see the organization's tax-exempt status threatened by certain things that local committees wanted to do. Or we would worry about the possibility of litigation against the organization should someone be hurt in some event.

Beyond our problems with the local committees, we often found ourselves in a struggle with "the regionals": regional committees responsible for organizing, coordinating, and supervising local committees. And there was also "the national committee," responsible for actually running the whole thing.

Looking from the other side, I knew that the local committees and others often complained about "the board." The board was a constant pain: on the one hand, demanding paperwork that seemed far removed from and irrelevant to the real business of visiting shut-ins and, on the other hand, being a wet blanket that dampened enthusiasm for really imaginative ideas. When one committee wanted to have a dinner-cruise-art-auction as a fund-raising activity, we said no, asking, "What if it loses money? Suppose someone falls overboard?" When a committee wanted to visit shut-ins on other holidays during the year, we asked that they concentrate their efforts on a major, national visit during Christmas and Hanukkah.

What's most distressing in all of this is that all parties were right, in a sense. I could see that from having participated in so many different parts of the whole. I was annoyed with "the board" when I was organizing a local team, and I was annoyed with the local folks when I was on the board. The locus of the problem was in the nature of social structure.

A number of remedies provide some relief in problems of this sort. Education is one example. Make sure that everyone in every part of the organization understands the needs and concerns of others. To the extent that the local committees could understand our need to file reports with the state of California to protect our tax-exempt status, the paperwork required of them was a little less odious. Communication is important. As parts of an organization isolate themselves from one another, they are headed for trouble.

The most effective solution I have ever been able to find, however, has to do with how we see and refer to each other. Specifically, when those of us on the board of directors stopped talking about "the national committee" and talked about Rita and Jim and Elizabeth, we had fewer problems. And the same was true when we were held as individual participants rather than "the board." When we dealt with each other as humans rather than as social statuses, we operated on the basis of our relationships and our love and admiration for each other. Referring to each other by our statuses, however, detached us from those ties and denied us the power those personal ties could provide.

Even realizing the power of this solution, I have always found it difficult to stick to it. I have always felt I was swimming upstream, and I constantly yield to the flow of talking and dealing with friends as organizational objects. It's a powerful force, but one that can be countered to some extent.

Strategy Versus Tactics

Here's another distinction that may be useful to you. When designing *strategy* for social action, aim at social structure. Always aim at institutional change when considering the long haul. Aim your *tactics* at individuals, however. This is similar to the slogan of many environmental groups today: Think globally, act locally.

Thus if your long-term aim were to restructure the American political process, you should pay special attention to social structural matters: how existing processes may support particular classes or interest groups, what elements of the situation relate to organizational survival, and so forth. When you are ready for action, however, remember that you can communicate only with other human beings. Communicate appropriately to achieve your purpose.

Pitting Organizations
Against Each Other

Sometimes it is appropriate to turn one segment of social structure against another. This can be risky, but sometimes this kind of escalation is all that works.

Years ago, when I was a graduate student, I joined a book club, as many of us do from time to time. I got a bunch of free books and incurred an obligation to buy a certain number of club offerings over the period of the next year. As the months rolled by, I purchased the requisite number of books, decided I didn't want to belong any more, and marked a monthly offering "Please cancel my membership." When the next month's offer arrived, I returned it with the same request. Then I began including letters asking that my membership be canceled. Nothing made any difference. My requests were simply ignored.

Eventually I wrote a letter that said I was canceling my membership and that I no longer was going to send back the monthly cards to refuse the monthly book offers. As a consequence of this decision, I began receiving the books I had not refused. At first, I marked the books "REFUSED. Return to sender." When I tired of that, I sent a letter to the club, announcing that I no longer would return the unwanted books.

Now, as the books arrived, I simply set them aside, unopened. Bills began arriving for ever-increasing amounts. I put them with the books.

Finally I received a letter from the club, announcing that I was greatly in arrears in paying for my books and that they were about to take serious action. They would turn my account over to a bill collector, and, among other things, this was going to seriously damage my credit rating.

At this point, I typed a full and careful letter to the club, recalling the long, sad history of my attempts to cancel my membership after having fulfilled my obligations to them. I indicated that I had not opened any of the books in question and that I would be willing to turn them over to the club if they wanted to send someone by the house, but I was no longer willing to take the trouble of mailing them back.

I made lots of copies of the letter. I sent a copy to each of my U.S. senators and one to my representative. Then I went to the library, found a directory of federal agencies, and began sending copies to any agency whose name seemed appropriate to my plight. For example, I sent a copy to the Interstate Commerce Commission and another to the Fair Trade Commission. I may have sent a copy to the FBI.

Each copy of my letter to the book club was accompanied by a note saying I was not an attorney nor could I afford to hire one, but I had been brought up to believe that in America the government would look out for the little guy—or words to that effect.

Each of these letters brought my situation to the attention of organizations, more than to the attention of individual human beings. I had no misconception that my senators or representative would ever know anything about my troubles with the book club, for example. Better than that, I was addressing their staffs: organizations with programmed purposes and procedures. You can imagine the warning lights flashing within the synapses of the Congressional social structure: "Constituent-in-distress! Constituent-in-distress!" My senators and representative, as individuals, were surely smart enough to recognize that helping me in this situation was going to have no appreciable effect on their chances for reelection. And although they may, as individuals, be genuinely committed to looking out for their constituents' needs, my particular problem was not the most deadly one occurring within their regions of responsibility. Fortunately I was dealing with social structure rather than humans. Each organization had been programmed to mobilize for war whenever a constituent seemed to be in trouble.

I sent my letter to the book club, plus all the copies. For a week, nothing happened. Then I received an avalanche of mail I had not expected. Everyone I wrote to acknowledged receiving my request and told me whom they had forwarded it to for action. Although I had not known who in government could help me, I had made contact with a network of organizations and statuses that were wired into each other.

Over the next few weeks, I received progress reports from various agencies, sometimes reporting that they had forwarded my case to an agency even more appropriate than they were.

It all came to a head, one day, when I received a 2-page non-form-letter from the New York City Post Office, Division of Fraud and Mailability. The letter informed me that agents Brown and Jones had driven out to Long Island, where the book club was located, and they had talked to Mrs. Smith, who was in charge of the club. Mrs. Smith had told them how sorry she was at my plight and asked them to pass her concerns on to me. Further, the book club wanted me to keep the unordered books as a token of their remorse for troubling me so, and I was simply to ignore any further correspondence that might reach me before she could get the flow turned off. That was the last I heard from the club.

CONCLUSION

I hope this final story illustrates the main theme of this book: We create social structure in order to make it possible for us to live together. For social structure to serve that purpose, however, it must persist, so we build survival mechanisms into it. Inevitably these mechanisms give social structure a life of its own, and when it needs modification and elimination to be appropriate to changing human circumstances, the survival mechanisms in social structure bring resistance to change. Very often, then, we think we are at odds with the social structures we created.

As social structure ages and puts a few generations between its human creators and those who follow, we tend to reify the social structure, making it something more sacred than a simple human agreement or casually established custom. Altering old social structure is much harder than altering the new crop.

I hope you have come to see that social structure is not intrinsically your enemy. It just is. How you deal with it is up to you. As we've just seen, you can be its victim or you can use it as a powerful tool.

You can forget about our space program, nuclear weapons, and genetic engineering. Our most powerful creation is the autopoietic social structure that makes our life together possible and also threatens to make it unworthy of who we really are. Whether our social structure will serve us or we it, however, is in our hands. Our biggest enemy is the belief that things are otherwise.

Points of Discussion

- What are some social problems that concern you? What do you suppose you could do to make a difference with regard to those problems?

- Can you recall times when you expressed concern about some social problem and were told that you were too young to understand how things really were? How did you react to that?

- If you were to become a sociologist, what kind of work do you think might be the focus of your career?

Reading Further

In *The Asymmetric Society* (Syracuse, NY: Syracuse University Press, 1982), James S. Coleman examines the creation of "corporate actors," the form in which social structure becomes embodied and interacts with humans. The classic example is the modern corporation, which is viewed in the same way as an individual human under much American law. Coleman's book provides excellent historical analyses of the phenomenon we've studied in this book.

Warren Bennis is a sociologist who has devoted much of his career to the nature and the problems of organizations. *The Unconscious Conspiracy: Why Leaders Can't Lead* (New York: American Management Associations, 1976) and *Why Leader's Can't Lead: The Unconscious Conspiracy Continues* (San Francisco: Jossey-Bass, 1989) lay out the difficulties of leadership in modern society. Bennis is committed to finding and communicating techniques for overcoming those problems.

Robert Jackall's *Moral Mazes: The World of Corporate Managers* (New York: Oxford University Press, 1988) offers insights into the dilemmas faced by those charged with responsibility for the survival of organizations.

Snell Putney's *The Conquest of Society* (Belmont, CA: Wadsworth, 1972) sounded an early warning about the danger of social structure developing a life of its own and converting humans into "servo-men." This witty and engaging book was clearly decades ahead of its time. It is out of print, but if you can find it, you are in for a special treat.

For more ideas on how to deal effectively with social structure and the problems of the world in general, you might enjoy my *You Can Make a Difference* (New York: St. Martin's, 1985). Much of the book is devoted to describing examples of individuals stepping forward to take charge of social problems they did not create.

REFERENCES

Aberle, D. F., Cohen, A. K., Davis, A. K., Levy, M. J., Jr., & Sutton, F. X. (1950). The functional prerequisites of a society. *Ethics, 9*(1), 100-111.

Babbie, E. (1985). *You* can *make a difference*. New York: St. Martin's.

Babbie, E. (1988). *The sociological spirit*. Belmont, CA: Wadsworth.

Babbie, E. (1992). *The practice of social research*. Belmont, CA: Wadsworth.

Barzun, J. (1991, March 20). We need leaders who can make our institutions companies of scholars, not corporations with employees and customers [Op-Ed section]. *Chronicle of Higher Education*, pp. B1-B2.

Bennis, W. (1976). *The unconscious conspiracy: Why leaders can't lead*. New York: American Management Associations.

Bennis, W. (1989). *Why leaders can't lead: The unconscious conspiracy continues*. San Francisco: Jossey-Bass.

Benseler, F., Heji, P. M., & Kock, W. K. (Eds.). (1980). *Autopoiesis, communication, and society*. Frankfurt, Germany: Campus Verlag.

Berger, P. (1963). *Invitation to sociology*. Garden City, NY: Doubleday.

Berger, P., & Luckman, T. (1966). *The social construction of reality*. Garden City, NY: Doubleday.

Brinton, C. (1953). *The anatomy of revolution*. London: Cape.

Brown v. Board of Education of Topeka, Kansas (1954).

Butterfield, H. (1960). *The origins of modern science*. New York: Macmillan.

California Christian Collegian. (1927, May).

California Christian Collegian. (1928, June).

California Christian Collegian. (1930, June).

California School of Christianity. (1921). *Catalog*. Los Angeles: Author.

California School of Christianity. (1923). *CEER*. Los Angeles: Author.

Chapman College. (1942). *Catalog*. Los Angeles: Author.

Chapman College. (1946). *Catalog*. Los Angeles: Author.

Chapman College. (1985). *Catalog*. Orange, CA: Author.

Chapman University. (1991). *Catalog*. Orange, CA: Author.

Clover, H. A. (1960). *An historical study of Hesperian College, Woodland, California, from 1861 to 1896*. Master's thesis, Chapman College, Orange, CA.

Coleman, J. S. (1982). *The asymmetric society*. Syracuse, NY: Syracuse University Press.

Data needed for historical file. (1943, August). *Chapman College Review*, p. 4.

Deskins, R. (1944). *CEER*. Los Angeles: Chapman College.

Dr. M: Freedom has its limits. (1991, May 25). *New Straits Times*, p. 1.

Dr. M warns of agents of Western countries. (1991, May 27). *New Straits Times*, p. 2.

Durkheim, E. (1951). *Suicide*. New York: Free Press. (Original work published 1897)

Ellul, J. (1964). *The technological society* (J. Wilkinson, Trans.). New York: Knopf. (Original work published 1954)

Etzioni, A. (1991/2, Winter). The *Responsive Community* platform. *Responsive Community*, pp. 4-6.

Federal Bureau of Investigation (FBI). (1990). *Crime in the United States*. Washington, DC: Government Printing Office.

Festinger, L., Riecken, H., & Schacter, S. (1956). *When prophecy fails*. Minneapolis: University of Minnesota Press.

Flores, F. (1991). *Offering new principles for a shifting business world*. Emeryville, CA: Business Design Associates.

Freud, S. (1961). *Civilization and its discontents* (J. Strachey, Ed. and Trans.). New York: Norton. (Original published 1930)

Furman v. Georgia 428 U.S. 153, 173 (1972).

Gall, J. (1988). *Systemantics: How systems really work and how they fail*. Ann Arbor, MI: General Systemantics.

Gans, H. J. (1971, July/August). The uses of poverty: The poor pay all. *Social Policy*, pp. 20-24.

Gregg v. Georgia 428 U.S. 153, 96 S. Ct. 2909, L. Ed. 859 (1976).

Gross, S. R., & Mauro, R. (1989). *Death and discrimination: Racial disparities in capital sentencing*. Boston: Northeastern Press.

Hannaway, J. (1989). *Managers managing: The workings of an administrative system*. New York: Oxford University Press.

Harrison, M. I. (1991, Fall). The politics of consulting for organizational change. *Knowledge and Policy: The International Journal of Knowledge Transfer*, 4(3), 92-107.

Hechter, M., Opp, K.-D., & Wippler, R. (Eds.). (1990). *Social institutions: Their emergence, maintenance, and effects*. Hawthorne, NY: Aldine.

Hunt, M. (1985). *Profiles of social research: The scientific study of human interactions*. New York: Russell Sage.

Jackall, R. (1988). *Moral mazes: The world of corporate managers*. New York: Oxford University Press.

Levin, J. (1993). *Sociological snapshots: Seeing social structure in everyday life*. Newbury Park, CA: Pine Forge.

Levitin, T., Quinn, R., & Staines, G. (1971). *Sex discrimination against the American working woman.* Ann Arbor: University of Michigan, Institute for Social Research.

Linton, R. (1936). *The study of man.* New York: Appleton-Century.

Lipset, S. M. (1963). *The first new nation: The United States in historical and comparative perspective.* New York: Basic Books.

Maslow, A. H. (1943). A theory of human motivation. *Psychological Motivation, 50,* 370-396.

Maturana, H. R. (1980). Man and society. In F. Benseler, P. M. Heji, & W. K. Kock (Eds.), *Autopoiesis, communication, and society* (pp. 11-32). Frankfurt, Germany: Campus Verlag.

Maturana, H. R., & Varela, F. J. (1980). *Autopoiesis and cognition.* Dodrecht, Netherlands: Reidel.

McCleskey v. Kemp 107 S.Ct. 1756 (1987).

Mills, C. W. (1959). *The sociological imagination.* Oxford, UK: Oxford University Press.

Morgan, G. (1986). *Images of organizations.* Beverly Hills, CA: Sage.

Naisbitt, J., & Aburdene, P. (1985). *Re-inventing the corporation.* New York: Warner.

Ng, B. (1991, May 16). Don't knock rules, they have made us what we are. *Straits Times* (Singapore), p. 26.

Parkinson, C. N. (1957). *Parkinson's law.* Boston: Houghton Mifflin.

Parsons, T. (1951). *The social system.* New York: Free Press.

Peter, L. J., & Hull, R. (1969). *The Peter principle.* New York: Bantam.

Plessy v. Ferguson 163 U.S. 537 (1896).

President's message. (1943, December). *Chapman College Review,* p. 2.

President's message. (1944, March). *Chapman College Review,* p. 2.

Putney, S. (1972). *The conquest of society.* Belmont, CA: Wadsworth.

Reeves, G. (1942, September 1). Association vital to college program. *Chapman College Alumnus,* pp. 1, 4.

Ritzer, G. (1993). *The McDonaldization of society.* Newbury Park, CA: Pine Forge.

Rosenberg, M. (1968). *The logic of survey research.* New York: Basic Books.

Secter, B. (1992, March 8). Checking into Doctor Hell. *Los Angeles Times Magazine,* pp. 16-18, 37-39.

Senge, P. M. (1990). *The fifth discipline: The art and practice of the learning organization.* Garden City, NY: Doubleday.

Short, J. F., Jr. (Ed.). (1986). *The social fabric.* Beverly Hills, CA: Sage.

Simmel, G. (1968). The conflict in modern culture. In K. P. Etzkorn (Ed. and Trans.). *Georg Simmel: The conflict in modern culture and other essays* (pp. 11-26). New York: Teachers College Press. (Original work published 1921)

Singh, J. V. (Ed.). (1990). *Organizational evolution: New directions.* Newbury Park, CA: Sage.

Sixty students in search of a campus. (1943, March). *Chapman College Review,* p. 1-5.

Sturgeon, T. (1953). *More than human.* New York: Farrar, Straus & Giroux.

Taylor, F. W. (1911). *Principles of scientific management.* New York: Harper & Row.

Tucker, Robert C. (1972). *The Marx-Engels Reader.* New York: W. W. Norton.

U.S. Bureau of the Census. (1991). *Statistical abstract of the United States.* Washington, DC: Government Printing Office.

Ulrich, H., & Probst, G. J. B. (Eds.). (1984). *Self-organization and management of social systems.* New York: Springer-Verlag.

University of California Regents v. Bakke (1978).

van de Vall, M. (1992, April). *Sociological practice in modern policy making: Supply and demand.* Revision of a paper presented at the Research Council Conference of the International Sociological Association (ISA), Onati, Spain.

von Foerster, H. (1984). Principles of self-organization—In a socio-managerial context. In H. Ulrich & G. J. B. Probst (Eds.), *Self-organization and management of social systems: Insights, promises, doubts, and questions* (pp. 2-24). New York: Springer Verlag.

Weber, M. (1946). Bureaucracy. In H. Gerth & C. W. Mills (Eds.), *From Max Weber: Essays in sociology* (pp. 196-264). New York: Oxford University Press. (Original work published 1925)

We won't compromise. (1991, May 26). *New Straits Times,* p. 1.

Wilson, E. O. (1978). *On human nature.* Cambridge, MA: Harvard University Press.

Zeleny, M. (1981).*Autopoiesis, A theory of living organizations.* New York: North Holland.